THE FAMILY CREATIVE WORK SHOP

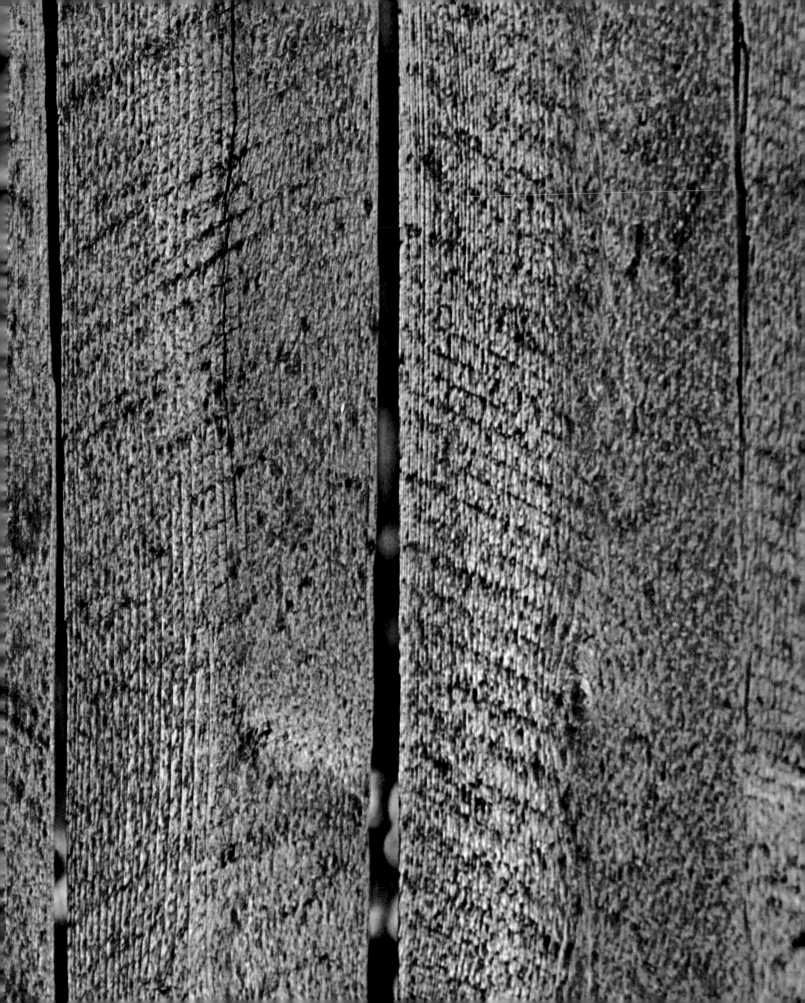

# THE FAMILY
# CREATIVE WORKSHOP

## 3

Boxes, Braided Rugs,
Breads, Bread Sculpture,
Brewing, Buttons,
Calligraphy, Cameras, Candlemaking,
Caning and Rushing,
Canoeing, Cardboard, Card Tricks

**Plenary Publications International, Inc.**
**New York and Amsterdam**

The Project-Evaluation Symbols appearing in the title heading at the beginning of each project have these meanings:

## Range of approximate cost:

¢ Low: Under $5, or free and found natural materials

$ Medium: About $10

$$ High: Above $15

## Estimated time to completion for an unskilled adult:

⌛ Hours

🕐 Days

📅 Weeks

## Suggested level of experience:

Child alone

Supervised child or family project

Unskilled adult

Specialized prior training

## Tools and equipment:

Small hand tools

Large hand and household tools

Specialized or powered equipment

## Publishers

Plenary Publications International, Incorporated, 300 East 40th Street, New York, 10016.

Allen Davenport Bragdon, Editor-in-Chief and Publisher of the Family Creative Workshop. President, Plenary Publications International, Inc.

Nancy Jackson, Administrative Asst. Wilson Gathings, Production Editor. Jackson Hand, Consulting Editor.

## Editorial Preparation

Wentworth Press, Incorporated,

Walter Ian Fischman, Director.
Jacqueline Heriteau, Editor.
Francesca Morris, Executive Editor.
Susan Lusk, Art Director.
Frank Lusk, Director of Photography.

## For this volume

Contributing editors: Barbara Auran-Wrenn, Edward Claflin, Len Corwen, Jo-Anne Jarrin, Jay Jonas, Ivan Kursar, Jane Miller, John Noblitt, Elizabeth O'Bryan, John Savage. Contributing illustrators: Barbara Auran-Wrenn, Herbert Jonas, Frank Lusk.

Contributing photographers: Gene Colangelo, Lionel Freedman, Ivan Kursar, Tom Yuen.

Materials for Boxes, courtesy of C.W. Stockwell Company. Photograph of old Hires sign, Brewing, courtesy of Hires Division, Crush International, Inc. Illuminated Manuscript page, Calligraphy, courtesy of the Spencer Collection of the New York Public Library, Astor, Lenox and Tilden Foundations. Old English and Chancery Cursive Letters, Calligraphy courtesy of Hunt Manufacturing Company, Speedball Division.

**On the cover**
Candles, cast in milk cartons and old tennis ball cans colored with crayons and commercial dyes. See the entry "Candles," beginning on page 314. Photograph by Paul Levin.

Published by Plenary Publications International, Incorporated, 300 East 40th Street, New York, N.Y. 10016, for the Blue Mountain Crafts Council.

Library of Congress Catalog Card Number: 73-89331. Complete set International Standard Book Number: 0-88459-021-6. Volume 3 International Standard Book Number: 0-88459-002-X.

Manufactured in the United States of America. Printed and bound by the W. A. Krueger Company, Brookfield, Wisconsin. Color separations by Lithotech, Incorporated, Orlando, Fla. Second Printing, 1974

# Contents

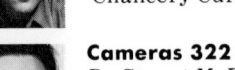
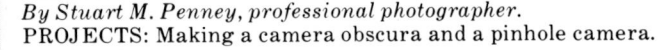

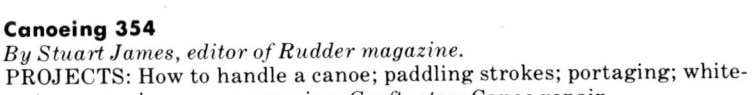

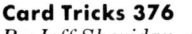

# BOXES

# Convert Your Discards

Boxes have held an obvious fascination for man ever since he began to accumulate possessions and needed something in which to store and carry them. Not content with simple, functional containers, he has crafted them of the finest materials and decorated them lavishly. Ornately painted Egyptian and Roman chests, jeweled French snuffboxes of the eighteenth century, and Victorian inlaid chests for silverware were cherished for their beauty as much as for their usefulness. The skilled work required to make a beautifully crafted box is a lost art today, but a little ingenuity can give an everyday box new life and new uses.

We have all had our own special boxes for childhood treasures, and at the top of the list was that handy cigar box of Dad's. What a perfect container— and with its own hinged lid! It seemed forever before the last cigar was smoked and the box finally became ours. We could find countless new uses for it.

Applying this not-so-modern method of recycling even more vigorously, today we can use all kinds of boxes in new and more attractive ways. Milk and cream containers, kitchen matchboxes, milk crates, carbonated-beverage crates, shoe boxes—throwaway items like these are excellent raw materials. In the past few years, I have turned all of these into useful and decorative objects. The milk and beverage crates are the most difficult to come by; but with some determination, you can get them from dairy and beverage companies, supermarkets, or community trash-disposal areas.

When you recycle containers, especially beverage crates, it is important to prepare them for their new role. Wash all surfaces with a strong detergent solution, using a stiff brush to loosen stubborn grease and grime. Remove all protruding nails or staples, and sand any wooden or metal surfaces that you plan to paint. Seal all raw wood with liquid sealer to keep it from absorbing too much paint. A little work with a hammer and nails will restore a shaky box to its original sturdy condition.

*Design student John Noblitt is very interested in ecology, especially the recycling of used containers. His imaginative box constructions are fine examples of what can be done with patience and ingenuity.*

## Paper Folding and Cutting
# Milk-crate desk and seat
$$ 🕐 🚶 ⚗

Constructing the desk and seat shown in the color photograph on page 265 requires a good deal of time and patience. However, the desk's large working surface and the moderate cost of this project make it well worth while. To cover the desk and seat, I combined two wallpaper patterns. I was careful to choose patterns with similar color schemes, for a coordinate effect.

These are the materials you will need: A stock-size (82 by 24 inches), unpainted, hollow-core door (or any narrow slab door); five milk crates; three single rolls of 27-inch-wide wallpaper in the pattern of your choice (the pattern should be of the nondirectional type, meaning that it will appear the same no matter what way it is turned); two rolls of wallpaper in a contrasting pattern for the insides of the milk crates; a box of wallpaper paste; a wallpaper-paste brush; a utility knife or a single-edge razor blade; three plastic undercabinet organizer drawers with runners and mounting instructions; a spray can of paint in a color to go with the basic color of the wallpaper; a spray can of clear, semigloss polyurethane; a two-tube unit of epoxy glue; a square of foam filler in a size to fit the end of one of

This desk was made by recycling a door and some everyday boxes. An old toy chest was transformed into a colorful bench. Directions for the bench are on page 269.

the milk crates; half a yard of fabric for the milk crate seat cushion (photographs, page 265); a staple gun and staples (or you may use upholstery tacks); a roll of decorative adhesive tape (or you may use two yards of braid trim). Follow these step-by-step instructions to make the desk top:

□ Mix the wallpaper paste according to the directions on the box, and seal one side and all edges of the door by brushing on a light coat of paste. Allow half an hour for paste to dry. To support the door while working on it, I stacked two crates, under each end, as they will be for the finished desk.

□ Measure the length of the door, and add twice its thickness, plus eight inches, to allow for a four-inch overlap at each end. The resulting figure is the length of wallpaper you should cut to cover the door on one side. My door measured 82 inches long and 1½ inches thick, so I cut a 93-inch length of 27-inch wide wallpaper. Don't cut off the selvage edge. You'll need it to overlap the door's width comfortably.

□ Brush the wallpaper with paste, and let it stand for 90 seconds.

□ Center the paper on the door, and smooth out the air bubbles with a soft cloth or towel, working from the center toward the edges (photograph 2). Small bubbles that remain will work themselves out as the paper dries.

□ Fold the overlap around the edges, and press it to the underside.

□ Smooth the paper on the edges of the door with the cloth, working from the center of each edge to the corners, and fold at the corners as shown in photograph 11, page 270. This shows covering a cigar box, but the same technique can be applied here. Cut the excess paper off at all four corners. Overlap the remaining paper, and press it on the underside of the door.

1: These are the raw materials that were used. Shown are hollow core door, cigar box, toy chest, milk crates, oil paint tube boxes, and various other boxes.

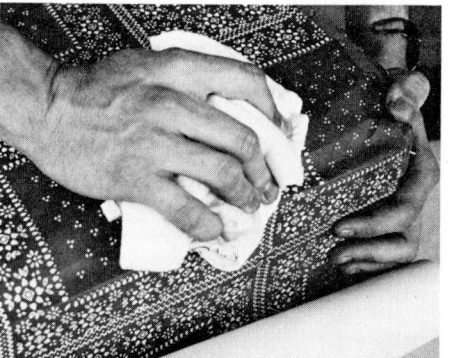

2: Press and smooth the wallpaper to the door and the crates with a soft cloth. Work from the center of the surface out, and then along the edges, as shown here.

3: Trim the wallpaper overlap on the crates with the utility knife. Don't cut the paper to fit exactly, but leave some overlap, which is later trimmed as shown.

□ When the wallpaper is thoroughly dry (no less than six hours), spray it with two coats of clear polyurethane. This will protect it from the scrapes and stains a desk top is normally subject to.

□ Spray-paint the drawers (all surfaces except front panels) and the runners. When paint is dry, center the drawers at the front on the underside of the door, and attach according to the manufacturer's directions. Use epoxy glue instead of screws, unless your door is of solid construction. Cut some wallpaper to fit, and paste it to the fronts of the drawers. For a neat appearance, align the wallpaper pattern on the drawers with that on the door. Trim excess with the razor blade.

To make the desk-top supports and the seat for the desk, follow this step-by-step procedure:

□ Spray-paint the metal edges of all five crates, using the color that was used on the drawers. Work on one crate at a time from this point on.

□ Seal the wood surfaces by brushing on one coat of wallpaper paste. Let it dry for half an hour.

□ Cover the two long sides and the bottom of the crate with one piece of wallpaper, so that the gaps in the crate between the sides and the bottom will be covered (photograph 2). Fold the two ends of the wallpaper over the edges of the crate opening.

□ Cover the two remaining ends of the crate with wallpaper. Cut both pieces large enough to be folded over the edge of the crate opening. Trim all excess with the razor blade (photograph 3). If some of the wallpaper ends curl up after drying, secure them again with a little epoxy glue.

□ For the crate seat (color photograph, right) proceed as directed above, but leave one end of the crate uncovered. Cut the square of foam filler to fit this end.

□ Measure and cut the fabric for the seat cover to the dimensions of the end of the crate, plus a four-inch overlap on all four sides.

□ Staple the fabric along the front underside of the crate (photograph 4). Pull the fabric taut over the foam, and staple it at the center only of the opposite side. Staple at the center of the remaining two sides, pulling the fabric tight.

□ Staple the corners of the fabric (photographs 5 and 6), then secure the remaining fabric ends with staples.

□ Cover the staples with decorative tape (photograph 7).

□ Cover all inside surfaces of the five crates with the contrasting paper.

□ Stack the four crates as shown in the color photograph, right, and rest the door on top of them. It isn't necessary, but if you like you can secure the crates to each other with screws. Don't secure the door, however, unless it is of solid wood.

This decorative desk and seat are covered with paper of a pattern also available in fabric for making drapes. The drawers–the plastic undercabinet kind designed for kitchens– are optional.

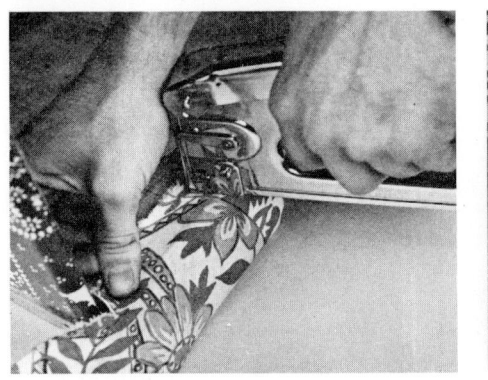

4: Staple fabric along inside edge of crate opening. Staples will be covered with paper that will line inside of crate. Notice cut in fabric to allow it to fit around corner of crate.

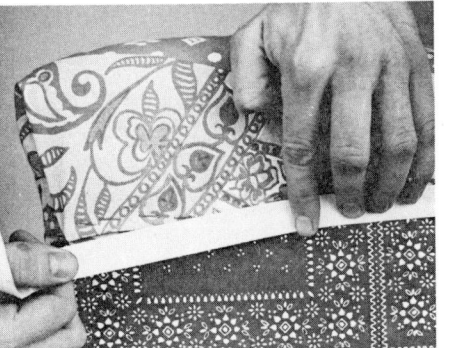

5: Pull the fabric tight, fitting it around the corner, and fold as in wrapping a package. Holding the fold aside, staple the fabric at the corner and about three inches in from the corner, as shown.

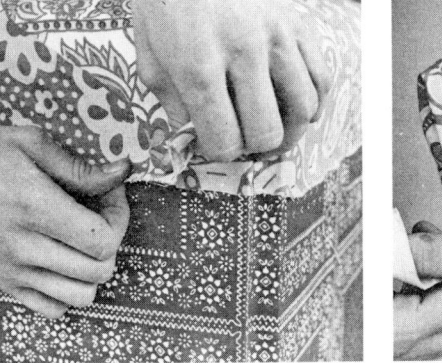

6: Finishing the fitted corner. Pull the fold down, and staple. Two back corners are fitted in this way. Two front corners, at crate opening, are fitted by simply turning fabric end in and stapling.

7: Cover the staples and the fabric ends with decorative adhesive tape. Choose a color that coordinates with the fabric and wallpaper. Any kind of decorative trim or braid would also serve.

Promising old boxes are everywhere to be found. Pick one up, carry it home, and give it a useful and decorative new life.

The current vogue for Americana includes this kind of beverage case. With almost nothing done to it, it can become a decorative, wall-mounted display case.

## Furniture and Refinishing
# Beverage-case curio cabinet

Carbonated-beverage cases like the one shown above are becoming increasingly difficult to find. This rarity adds to their interest and value, so if you do run across one, hold on to it. Use it as a sock or yarn holder, as a wine-bottle or spice-jar rack, or for an arrangement of small potted plants. You can think of other imaginative uses that will suit your practical or decorative needs.

I made a curio cabinet out of mine by painting the inside with flat black paint and hanging the case on a wall. It is supported by two nails which easily fit through the two openings between the crate slats. Hung this way, it serves as a convenient display case for small mementos or curios, or as a bookcase for paperbacks.

## Paper Folding and Cutting
# Kitchen-matchbox organizer ¢ ⧖ ⚇ ⛾

Straightening up the clutter of a messy drawer is always a problem, but you can solve that problem permanently with an organizer like the one below. It was very simply constructed from empty kitchen matchboxes. You can make one exactly like it, or you can vary the design, colors, and number of boxes to suit your taste and needs. You could also add quart milk cartons, cut to the height of the matchboxes.

To make an organizer like this one, you will need seven large kitchen matchboxes; a can of spray paint in the color of your choice; a small tube of glue; a roll of vinyl tape; enough wallpaper or decorative adhesive paper to cover the bottoms of the boxes; and a spray can of liquid polyurethane. Follow these instructions:

□ Spray-paint all the boxes, inside and out, and let the paint dry.
□ Turn the boxes bottom up, and arrange them as pictured or in a pattern of your own. Join them by crisscrossing vinyl tape in all directions over the bottom of the arrangement.
□ Turn the organizer over, and fold strips of tape lengthwise over the adjacent box edges, to hold the boxes firmly together.
□ Trim all outer edges with tape in the same manner.
□ Cut some scrap wallpaper to fit the inside bottoms of the boxes, and glue it on. Or line the bottoms with adhesive paper.
□ Spray all surfaces of the finished organizer with clear polyurethane. This isn't a must, but it helps protect the boxes from wear and tear.

A tidy drawer organizer like this one is easy to make with kitchen matchboxes or cut-down quart milk cartons. Instructions for making it are complete on this page.

## Paper Folding and Cutting
# Box wall sculpture

A good way to make use of those gift boxes that have been crowding your closet shelves, and to give full vent to your creativity, is to construct a wall sculpture like the one at the left. Grouping boxes this way offers endless free-form sculptural possibilities, any of which would add a colorful touch to a contemporary setting.

Boxes or box covers of any size qualify. I used everything from tiny matchboxes to large gift boxes. They are all mounted bottom side up and one on top of another on a ½-inch-thick plywood board. This board measured 24 by 36 inches, but you can use whatever size you wish. Keep things in proportion, though, by arranging mostly large boxes on large mounts, and small boxes on small mounts.

Materials you will need are a piece of plywood or heavy cardboard; assorted boxes and box covers; spray paint in whatever colors you choose; and white all-purpose glue. Follow these directions to assemble the sculpture:

This abstract wall hanging was made from a variety of boxes and box covers. You can make similar free-form designs by following the instructions on this page.

8: Applying glue to the edges of one of the boxes. Be careful not to let excess glue show on the outside of the box when it is applied to the sculpture.

9: Pressing a box in place. Notice that it rests only partially on boxes beneath. Use imaginative groupings—avoid a perfectly symmetrical arrangement.

□ Arrange the boxes in various ways on the mounting board until you find a design you like. Some of the boxes can overlap the edge.
□ Plan the color pattern, and mark each box with the initial of the color it is to be painted.
□ Make a sketch to refer to as you work.
□ Spray-paint the mounting board white or any color you believe will provide an attractive background for the colors of the boxes.
□ Spray-paint the outside of all the boxes, and let them dry.
□ Apply glue to the edges of the boxes that will form the first layer (photograph 8), and press them onto the board.
□ Glue the remaining boxes on top of the first ones. The finished sculpture will be more interesting if you place some of the boxes only partially on those beneath (photograph 9).

When all the glue has set, your sculpture will be ready to hang.

## Furniture and Refinishing
# Toy-chest bench

Somewhere in almost every household is a neglected toy chest, its former luster faded, and its youthful comrades grown up and long departed. Before you discard it or banish it to the attic, try a little rejuvenation. I turned one into the bench with storage compartment shown below and on page 262. You can do the same with any kind of chest with a hinged lid.

You will need the following materials besides the bench: sandpaper; two cans of spray paint in the color of your choice (or you may use a pint of brush-on paint); a roll of 1-inch decorative adhesive tape; a piece of foam padding the size of the chest's lid; enough fabric to cover the lid, taking into account its thickness, plus two inches extra on all sides to wrap under the lid; a staple gun and staples (or upholstery tacks). Follow this step-by-step procedure:

□ Wash and lightly sand the chest. Be sure to remove any loose paint.

□ Paint all surfaces except the top, and set the chest aside to dry.

□ When the paint is dry, apply the tape in the design shown below and in figure A. Measuring with a tape measure or ruler, and marking the point where the stripes will meet the top and bottom of the box before you apply the tape will ensure equal spacing between the stripes. The tape design shown here is only a suggestion. You can copy it exactly or create a design of your own.

□ Measure and cut the foam padding to fit the size of the chest's lid.

□ Cut and fit the fabric over the foam filler and chest lid. Follow the directions given on page 265 for upholstering the seat for the milk-crate desk. The only exceptions in this instance are that the fabric should be wrapped around all lid edges, cut out at hinges, and stapled underneath.

Another solution for recycling an old toy chest would be to cover it entirely with fabric, or wallpaper as was the door and crate desk on page 262.

Figure A: The angled stripes continue in the same direction on all sides of the chest.

A toy chest becomes a bench with its own storage compartment. Some paint, tape, and a cushioned lid give an old chest a useful new life.

### Furniture and Refinishing
# Decorative boxes

$ ☒ 🧍 🦶

Cigar boxes provide the perfect raw material to make two eye-catching decorative boxes.

### Studded Velvet Box

To make this box, you will need: a cardboard cigar box; half a yard of cotton velvet in a color you like; a small bottle of white, all-purpose glue; a small artist's paintbrush; a utility knife; 70 upholstery tacks in any metal finish; a hammer. Follow these steps:
□ Measure and cut a piece of velvet large enough to cover the bottom and sides of the box, plus an inch extra to fold over the lips of the three sides of the box opening.
□ Dilute a small amount of glue by mixing two parts glue to one part water. Apply a thin coat, with the paintbrush, to the outside bottom and four sides of the box. Let the glue dry until it is tacky to the touch.
□ Apply the fabric immediately by centering it on the bottom of the box and smoothing it from the center out. Work it over the sides, and smooth it to the corners (photograph 10).
□ Fold the fabric at the corners (photograph 11), and cut off the excess with the utility knife.
□ Apply glue to the lip of one of the sides; wait two or three minutes; then press the fabric along the lip (photograph 12). Do the same on the remaining two sides of the box. Don't glue the fabric to the inside. On the side attached to the lid, glue fabric up to the lid's hinge crease only.
□ Trim the fabric on all inside edges and at the hinge crease of the lid.
□ Cut a square of velvet to fit, and glue it to the outside of the lid only. Trim edges with the knife.
□ Push upholstery tacks into lid, following my pattern or any pattern of your own design. Use finger pressure, supporting the lid underneath with your other hand. Press, don't hammer, the tack points at right angles down into the inside of the cardboard lid, using the head of the hammer.

### Pheasant-Feather Box

To make the feather box, you will need these materials: a wooden cigar box; a yard-long sewn rope of pheasant breast feathers; a small bottle of white, all-purpose glue; a small artist's paintbrush; five round silver-colored knobs from a hardware store. The feathers can be obtained at a hobby shop or a display supply house. If you have difficulty finding feathers, you might strip an old feather-covered hat or use the eye part of peacock feathers from a florist shop. Follow these directions (opposite):

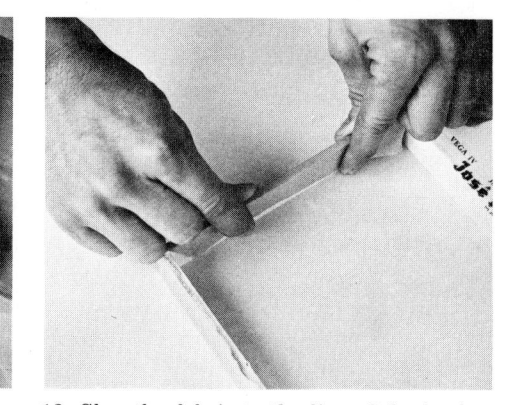

Figure B: Pattern of upholstery tacks. You can copy this design, or make up your own.

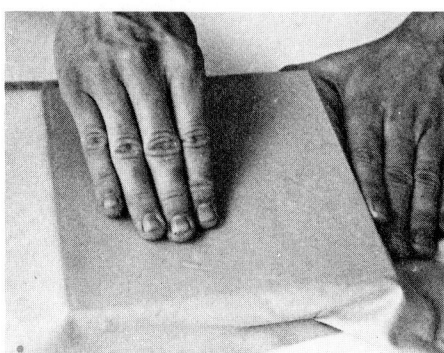

10: Glue the fabric to the bottom of the box, smoothing it out from the center. Press it down the sides, and smooth it toward the corners.

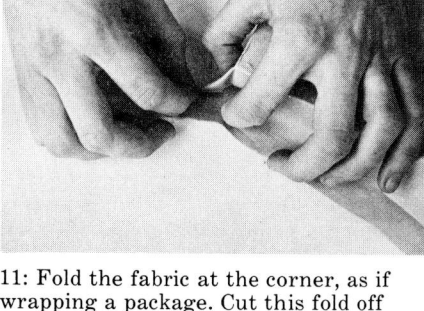

11: Fold the fabric at the corner, as if wrapping a package. Cut this fold off straight down along the corner edge of the box. Do this at all four corners.

12: Glue the fabric to the lips of the box's three sides. Cut off the excess along the inside edge. Do not glue fabric to the inside; trim it off instead.

These elegant accessories were once two ordinary cigar boxes. The directions are so simple they may inspire you to make these and more like them.

□ Free the feathers from the rope (photograph 13).
□ Apply diluted glue to a small area starting at the bottom of the sides. Refer to the velvet-box directions opposite for diluting the glue. Don't cover a large area—the glue would dry before you could cover it completely with feathers.
□ Lay feathers on small glued areas. Lay all feathers in the same direction, slightly overlapping them, and work toward the top of the box.
□ Place feathers on the top in the same manner, starting at the corners and working toward the center (photograph 14). Leave the bottom of the box uncovered, since it ordinarily will be hidden from view.
□ Screw the round knobs into the box at the four corners of the bottom and at the center front of the lid (see photograph 15 and color photograph above).

For related projects and crafts, see the entries "Cardboard," "Decoupage," and "Supergraphics."

13: Removing the feathers from the rope. Clip as close as possible to the stitches that hold the feathers together. You will need less than a yard of feathers to cover the box, but it is usually necessary to buy at least that amount.

14: Apply glue and feathers to the box in one small area at a time. Position the feathers so that they overlap, radiating from the center of the box top down the sides to the bottom edge.

15: Apply four knobs on the bottom corners and one in the front center of the lid. The legs and lid handle on this box are spheres, but you can use knobs in whatever shape you like. They screw easily by hand into the soft wood.

# Making New from Old

*Michelle Lester is a nationally known weaver and designer. Her handmade rugs, wall hangings, and fiber sculptures have been exhibited throughout the United States and have won numerous awards. She teaches textile design at the Fashion Institute of Technology, in New York City, and the Brooklyn Museum Art School.*

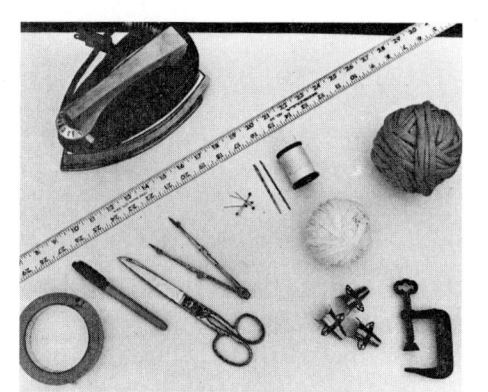

1: Braiding projects require scissors, compass, ruler, marking pencil, masking or cellophane tape, needle and pins, carpet thread, iron, C clamp, fabric cut into strips and sewn into long lengths, and, for large projects, metal braid aids.

Braiding is a simple way to plait fibrous materials into heavy strands, which can then be made into useful household items. Braids of strips from old clothes and remnants were used effectively by Colonial Americans, who fashioned them into oval or circular mats, spiraling the braided strands from a central curl until all available material was used.

In Colonial times, cloth could only be imported from England at exorbitant prices or be handloomed, so valuable worn cloth was reused in many ways. Warm woolen cloth was especially at a premium during the bitter New England winters. When it had provided protection to the struggling pioneers as garments, later cut down for children, and the garments had finally worn out, the heavy, insulating qualities of braided wool cloth, in its final phase, gave warmth underfoot. Lovely color patterns were developed for rugs by combining faded and redyed cloth, and certain color sequences were established and carried on as a folkcraft.

Today a great variety of materials, in many colors and patterns, is readily available, but the concept of recyling outgrown or scrap fabric is still appealing. Used fabrics often contribute softer colors and textures than do new fabrics, and new and used can be combined. Equipment for most braiding projects consists of simple household and sewing tools, although electric scissors and a sewing machine make shorter work of preparing fabric strips. There are even mail-order sources of inexpensive sturdy fabrics and precut strips of woven and knitted goods.

In general, the look of braided things is casual, making them best suited to country settings, recreation areas, and children's rooms, but choices of materials and color influence the final effect, so that unusual braided designs may be used in formal settings. The projects presented here will show how simple it is to make a braided shape, and how to plan practical projects and make unusual designs, using paper patterns.

## Preparing Materials

Fabrics of different types may be used together, but combine only those goods in one project that need the same care and are of the same weight. A sewing scrap or purchased remnant usually should be washed before work begins, to test its colorfastness and shrink-resistance, but a used fabric has probably been washed enough to ensure that it will neither run nor shrink. Some fabrics must be dry-cleaned and should be used for something that does not need frequent cleaning.

In choosing colors, lay out the remnants or partly worn clothing available, and decide which colors and textures complement one another. Remember that patterned fabrics will appear speckled in the many twists they will take, so patterns can be combined. I have found, however, that the braids have an especially fresh, crisp look if at least one solid-color strand is included in each combination of three strands.

Fabric weight influences the bulk of each braid and the thickness of the finished product, so similar weights work best together. To be sure your materials are suited to one another and to the project, make short sample braids, following individual project directions. Braid somewhat loosely, as you will in the final work, to allow for spiraling and turning into shapes. If the braid seems too thick, try another sample

Taping a contemporary braided rug made of discarded knits is the last step before sewing. The techniques for making this mat are borrowed from the Colonial Americans. Project instructions begin on page 278.

with narrower strips; if too thin, cut wider strips. These experiments will often help you find the proper thickness, but if results are still not satisfactory, try fabric of other weights.

### How To Cut

Cut all the clean fabric into strips of proper width. With woven goods, the cuts should be on the bias, or diagonal to the grain of the weave. Fold fabric as in figure A, to establish the proper diagonal: a 45-degree angle. If you are using a garment for strips, cut it first into flat sections, discarding useless collars, cuffs, and any other detailing. Open hems to lie flat. If material is woven, find the thread directions, and cut bias strips as in figure A. When all cloth of one color has been cut into even widths, sew ends of the strips together to make very long pieces, and gently roll the strips into balls of convenient size.

Many knits tend to stretch several ways, so they needn't be cut in any particular direction. Jersey slacks, for instance, could be cut in a gradual spiral down the legs, providing they are seamless or have tiny seams.

### Suppliers

If supplies are not available locally, here are a few mail-order sources:

Berry's of Maine, 20-22 Main Street, Yarmouth, Maine 04096 (wools, strip cutters, accessories, heavy threads, books).

The Fabric Shop, Route 53, Pembroke, Mass. 02359 (wools, kits, accessories).

Nu-flex Co., 246 First Avenue South, St. Petersburg, Fl. 33701 (wool strips, kits, accessories).

Tinkler & Co., Inc., P.O. Box 17, Norristown, Pa. 19404 ( jersey strips).

A

Figure A: Bias cuts follow a 45-degree angle from straight grain (direction of fabric threads) in woven goods. Angle is found by folding material as shown.

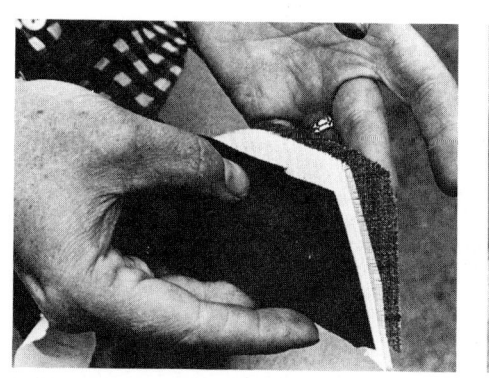

2: Place three bias-cut cotton strips with points together. These tapered ends will allow a few narrow beginning twists, which are easier to sew under than blunt ends, especially in making small items.

3: Clamp the three strips tightly to a table or chair back, using a C clamp. Small pieces of cardboard between clamp and furniture will prevent marring it. Or close strips in a drawer to hold them.

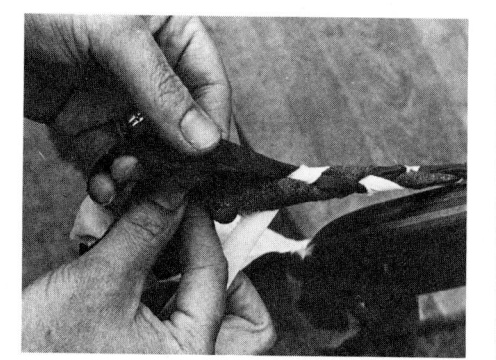

4: The first few twists of braid are made close to points of the strips. Turn the raw edges of the fabric in toward each other just before you twist them. This minimizes fraying of the cloth.

5: Maintain a slight tension to keep the braiding even; but be careful not to pull too tightly, as this would make it difficult to turn the braid into circular form. The braids should be flexible.

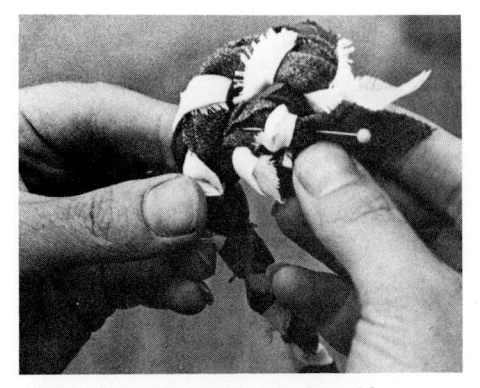

6: The first turns of finished braid are made into a tight circle and pinned into place, with the three fabric tips on the wrong side. Begin spiraling, with braid flat and edges touching.

7: With carpet thread, stitch on wrong side, as in this example of a coaster (see below), catching the edge of each round alternately. Ease the braid around the edge as you work so coaster lies flat.

For Deirdre Synek, age 12, braiding a set of four red-white-and-blue coasters to go under her family's iced-tea mugs was a project that required only an afternoon.

8: When coaster is the proper size, trim the ends to points and turn to wrong side. Fan out the points, to prevent bulkiness, and stitch down firmly. Coaster should be even and round.

9: Press the coasters lightly with a steam iron or a dry iron and damp press cloth. Be sure the coasters lie flat, to support glasses firmly. If they don't, cut stitches, and sew again, more loosely.

## Weaving, Braiding, Knotting
# Braided coasters

To make four coasters, you need about half a square yard of each of three fabrics in your choice of colors. They can be sewing square remnants or material from worn out or outgrown clothing. Absorbent fabrics are best. Cut the material into strips about 1¼ inches wide. Sew them end to end, as explained on the opposite page. For each coaster, you'll need three strands, each about 36 inches long—48 inches long for bigger coasters. Follow the step-by-step procedure given below and as shown in the photographs on this page to make the coasters:

Gather the pointed ends of the three strips, and clamp securely (see photograph 3). Using a three-strand braid, as shown in figure B, begin braiding close to the clamped points. Keep the braid twists loose; pull on the strands only enough to keep braiding even.

Pin both ends of the completed braid temporarily, and begin shaping. Curl one end into a small, tight circle; pin flat, with pointed ends underneath. Lead the braid around this circle, keeping it flat, for one round. Stitch together, catching touching sides of braid alternately and including the points. Ease another round into place; pin if necessary, and stitch. Don't tug the braid; if you do, it won't lie flat. Continue until the work is coaster size. As you work, check for size and roundness—incomplete rounds make a slightly oval shape. Add another round if it is needed. Cut off excess braid, tapering the ends. Turn these points to the underside, and stitch down securely. Press the finished coaster, following directions for photograph 9.

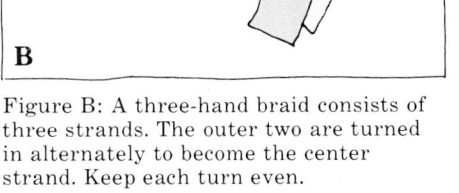

**B**

Figure B: A three-hand braid consists of three strands. The outer two are turned in alternately to become the center strand. Keep each turn even.

These braided placemats are easy to shape if you tape the braids to a paper guide. Combining plain and patterned sewing scraps makes this an inexpensive project. The placemats are miniatures of the braided oval rugs our grandmothers made.

## Weaving, Braiding, Knotting
# Braided place mats

The time-honored oval used in braided rugs is an ideal shape for place mats. Simply cut the strips a little narrower to make thinner braids and smaller ovals. Four yards of 36- to 42-inch wide material will give you four mats. Washable fabrics are a practical choice, and plain and patterned fabrics can be combined to complement tableware. The mats at the left were made of checked gingham, plain green and white cottons, and a leafy floral print on a white ground. To complete the mats, you will also need a large sheet of paper, ruler, compass, tape, marking pen, needle, and strong thread.

Make a pattern on the sheet of paper by drawing circles about an inch larger all around than your dinner plates. Photographs 10 and 11 show the steps; figure C diagrams complete oval pattern. For lightweight fabric such as gingham, cut strips 1½ inches wide; for heavier fabrics, such as poplin, cut strips 1 inch to 1¼ inches wide. (Note: Experts often stitch several different patterns of fabric end to end in each strip.) Now make long braid and begin shaping your mat.

Lay out the design by lightly taping the braids to the paper pattern with the face of the mat against the paper (photograph 12). Use small bits of tape at intervals. When the mat has grown to about 6 inches in width, complete a round; cut the braid, turn points back toward the center of the mat, and tape. Introduce two or three rounds of contrasting braid (photograph 13), and again lay ends toward center and tape. Return to the original coloring for enough rounds to come within an inch from the edge of your pattern. Finish with a few rounds of accent colors.

After the layout is complete, make sure all braid ends are on the surface facing you, and begin to stitch the braids in place, starting at the center. Remove the finished placemat from its paper pattern, and steam press it, or dampen it and press with a warm dry iron. As you press, block the mat into a perfect oval by pulling the edges slightly. If necessary, check its shape against the paper pattern.

Elaine Latham used traditional color sequences in this braided rug, which is made entirely of wool. Instructions for making it are on the opposite page.

◄ 10: Size of placemats depends on the dishes to be used with them. Put a plate face down on drawing paper; center compass (often, plate's center is marked by a tiny dot of glaze), and draw a circle. Allow an inch extra all around.

▼11: With compass set to same radius, use edge of first circle as center for the second. Join the interlocked shapes with straight lines at top and bottom and add a line from center to center.

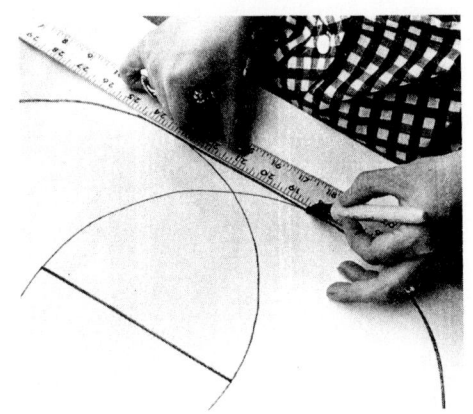

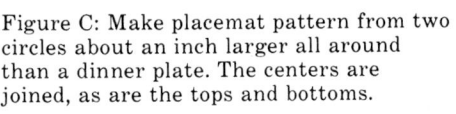

Figure C: Make placemat pattern from two circles about an inch larger all around than a dinner plate. The centers are joined, as are the tops and bottoms.

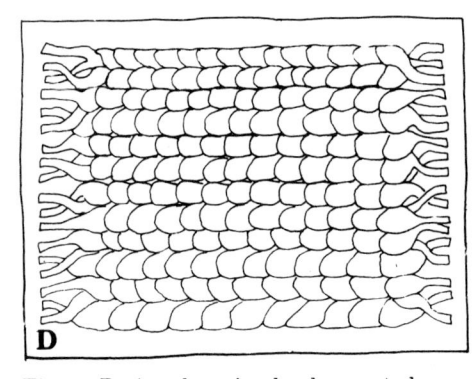

12: Begin by taping first braid above and below center mark. Ease plenty of extra braid into the sharp turns, especially near the mat's center. This prevents the growing oval shape from buckling.

13: As the mat grows, add rounds of new color combinations where they seem desirable. Use bits of tape frequently as sharp curves are shaped. If the work buckles, pull up braid, and lay it again.

Figure D: Another simple placemat shape is a rectangle, with short lengths of braid filling the pattern in parallel rows. The ends can be stitched invisibly.

**Weaving, Braiding, Knotting**
# Traditional braided rug

The traditional oval rug pictured opposite was made by a native New Englander, Elaine Latham. She follows a time-honored formula for coloring the beautifully made rugs that decorate her Early American home. New colors are introduced, one at a time, so that color changes are very gradual. Dark shades at the outside edge make the rug appear flat, and interesting colors at the center focus attention.

Decide dimensions, and subtract the width from the length. The remainder is the length of the starting braid. Use coating wool in 1½- to 2-inch strips Cut lighter weight wool wider, or tuck an extra strip inside the light one as filler. Allow ¾ of a pound of wool per square foot of rug. Turn in raw edges of strips as you braid. No taping is necessary; sew rounds in place with carpet thread. Tuck in ends, and sew tightly, to make the rug reversible.

## Weaving, Braiding, Knotting
# Petal-design rug

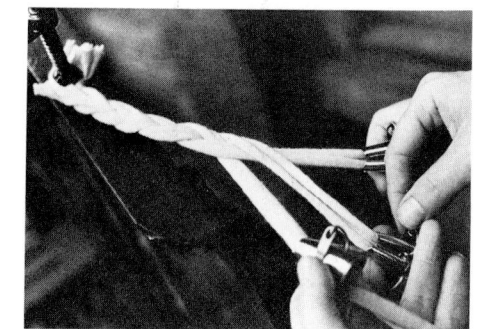

14: Metal braid aids guide heavy fabrics into neat rolls, with edges tucked in. Aids are especially helpful when you braid heavy fabrics for a rug.

About 9 pounds of cotton-jersey strips were enough to make the petal-design rug below. Cut knit goods yourself, or purchase precut strips, or use woven goods as in previous projects. Choose about 8 pounds of goods in colors that will blend into a predominant tone for the rug. The remainder of the material should provide an accent color for defining the center and border. For rug-making, you may want to purchase small metal cones equipped with tension devices, designed to help heavy strips curl neatly into the braids (see photograph 14). Several brands are available in needlework shops or from the sources listed on page 274.

On a piece of paper 4 feet square, draw a circle 16 inches in diameter, and another 45 inches in diameter, using the same center. To draw large circle, attach a pencil to the end of a string and pivot it around a push pin. Space six radii equally around the circles. Following the steps in figure E, lay braid in the center circle with tape, as described earlier. With main rug color, fill the shape within half an inch of its edge. Next, use the accent braid to outline the circle, and, at the same time, form the dividing shapes that protrude about 6 inches along the radii. To fill in petals, work from the outside of each petal toward the center. The unusual

The unusual petal design of this rug was first planned and shaped on paper. Unique contemporary designs are easy to make with this method.

shape will be easier to fill in this way. You may have to pull up the taped braid at times, to adjust it to fit the difficult turns in the spiral. Keep the braid as flat as possible. The next accent rings must indent deeply between the rounded petals to fill in gaps. As you put the final rounds in place, only a slight indentation is needed. This gives the rug an interesting but practical silhouette. If indentations were too deep, the edges might curl or be caught up under foot. To make the rug reversible, tuck the ends of the braids or colors carefully into neighboring twists and stitch them securely. Figure F shows a method of tucking in ends, and an alternative technique—butting ends together.

Once you have completed one of the braided projects shown here, you may want to design your own. Designs can be adapted from floral motifs or geometric patterns, simplified to suit the braiding technique. Color plays a primary role. Remember that it contributes both hue and value. Hue is the family of the color—red, blue, green. Value is its lightness or darkness. A light blue strand in an otherwise dark braid has an effect much different from a royal or navy blue. Dark blues give the whole braid a darker appearance, and the braid's effect in the total design is a strong, dark line. Light blue, however, will create regular, distinct spots as it twists its way in and out of the braid, making a dotted line in the design. In the same way, a braid of three entirely different values appears even more like a broken line. All these variations can create pleasing effects and are useful in developing patterns.

Broken color lines are good transitional patterns. When you introduce a bold color change, a useful trick is to add the new color first as one part of a preceding round. The traditional formulas for introducing new colors make the transitions even more gradual, as in the rug pictured on page 276.

Unusual materials often suggest projects: rope and twine, nubby silks, raffia, and ribbons may provide inspiration. For related projects and crafts, see "Colonial Crafts," "Hooked Rugs," "Rag Rugs," "Rya," and "Weaving."

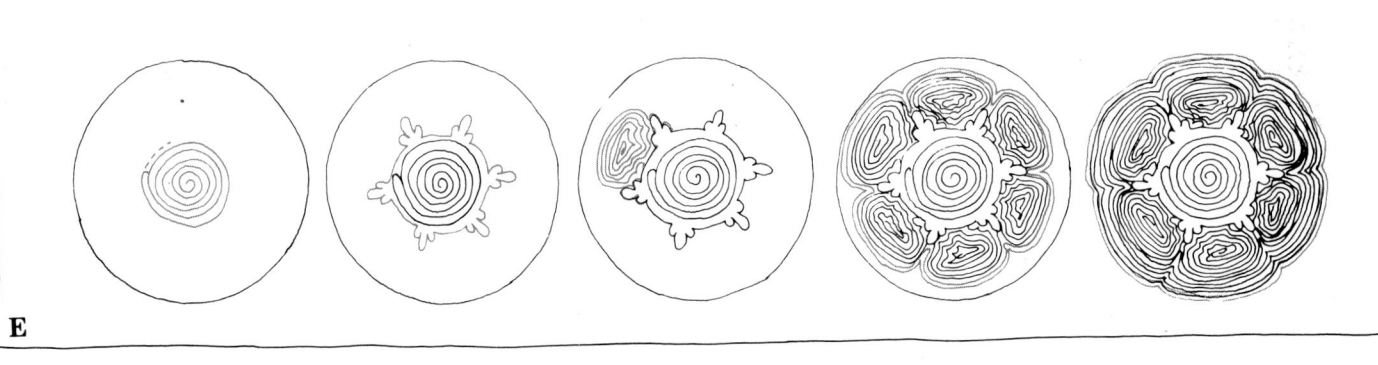

E

Figure E: The five steps in shaping the petal rug are sketched here: Filling the central circle with the main color; adding an accent outline with six spokes to begin petals; filling each petal with the main color from outline toward the center; circling the petals with accent color— indenting to fill gaps between petals; and finishing with smoother rounds of mixed colors. Tape whole plan before sewing.

▶ Figure F: At right are two methods for joining braids in the work: The three ends may be tucked into neighboring braid to make a tapered finish (bottom), or the ends of two meeting braids can be tucked into themselves to make blunt ends, which are then butted together and stitched (top). Tapering must be used for final round.

F

# BREADS
# Bannock to Sourdough

The best bread from the best bakery doesn't have as much appeal as crisp, golden, homemade loaves. Most homemakers who find romance in old ways have experimented with raised (leavened) breads, the type our grandmothers made in farm kitchens long ago, but little attention has been given to trail breads. These are the breads cowboys, goldminers, and pioneers cooked over open campfires in the days when Americans were discovering America.

Corn pone (fried corn bread) and bannock (a flat cake of oatmeal or other grain) are famous griddle-fried breads. Though bannock is Scottish, the name is also given to similar bread made by American Indians. Simple bannock and corn pone are unleavened, but leavened breads can also be pan-fried. Try the trail-bread recipes on pages 282 and 283 the next time you go camping. The smell of bread cooking in the open over a fire is a very special treat.

The most famous pioneer bread is sourdough. This dough, by the way, makes wonderful pancakes, muffins, and pizza crust. Sourdough was the staff of life for the 1849 goldminers and gave them the name by which they still are known. Why it is called sourdough and how it is handled are discussed in the section that begins on page 285.

◄Frank Yuen fries bannock, one of the historic trail breads described on page 282.

Dry ingredients for trail breads are premixed, bag-packed, as those shown here. Fresh milk and butter are optional. Premixed ingredients include dry milk so recipe can be made with plain water. Bacon fat or oil can be used if butter is unavailable.

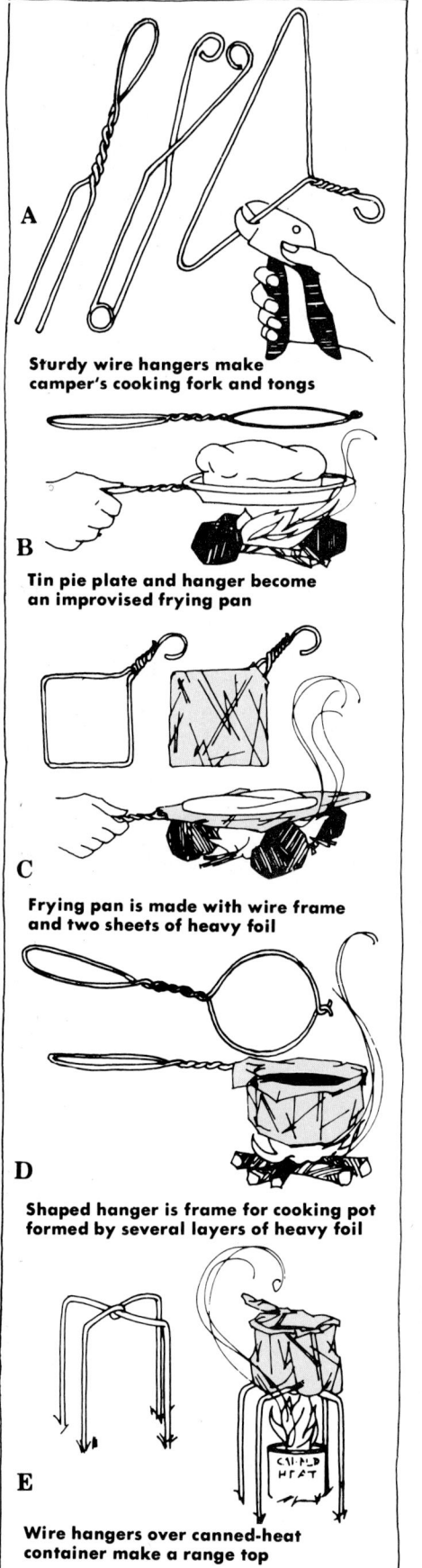

**Sturdy wire hangers make camper's cooking fork and tongs**
*(A)*

**Tin pie plate and hanger become an improvised frying pan**
*(B)*

**Frying pan is made with wire frame and two sheets of heavy foil**
*(C)*

**Shaped hanger is frame for cooking pot formed by several layers of heavy foil**
*(D)*

**Wire hangers over canned-heat container make a range top**
*(E)*

## Kitchen Favorites and Celebrations
# Trail breads

Any type of bread, including the sourdough bread described on page 289, can be cooked over a campfire; but yeast-raised breads are more difficult to handle successfully in the open air because yeast's ability to raise dough depends on a warm, draftless environment. Easier are yeastless griddle-fried breads, such as bannock and corn pone, for which recipes are given here.

Bannock traditionally is the bread of the wilderness traveler, and it can be prepared innumerable ways. The simplest bannock is a baked or fried mixture of oatmeal or white or whole-wheat flour, salt to taste, and enough water to form a thick dough.

The simplest corn pone is made with yellow corn meal, a bit of salt, and enough water to form a loose dough. The flavor is rather flat, and the texture is gritty; but like the simple bannock, it is good if you have been without bread of any kind for a couple of days.

The recipes given here for Bannock with Baking Powder and for Corn Pone are a little more complex than the simple wilderness concoctions, but no harder to make at your campsite if you premix the dry ingredients before you leave home. Sealed into plastic bags a size larger than sandwich bags, they add little weight to the trail pack, keep forever almost, and as a bonus, the plastic bag serves as a mixing bowl when it is time to add the milk or water that turns these ingredients into dough.

### Cooking Camp Breads

When you are going to griddle-cook trail bread, it is important that the campfire be at the right heat before you mix the dough. Generally it takes at least 15 minutes for a fire to burn down to the glowing-embers state that makes the low heat a griddle bread requires. Preheat the frying pan or griddle before adding the batter, and protect the frying bread with foil set to windward, as shown in photograph 3,

Frying isn't the only way to cook trail breads. They can be baked in various camp cooking devices, such as the popular reflector oven, which does a fine job but is a bit heavy for backpacking. Trail breads can also, in an emergency, be cooked on a heated rock and in any improvisation of the enclosed space of an oven you can think of. You can devise a surprising amount of useful equipment from coat hangers, as shown at left.

### Bannock with Baking Powder

1½ cups all-purpose unsifted flour
2 teaspoons baking powder
2 teaspoons sugar
1 teaspoon salt
2 tablespoons powdered milk

1 tablespoon melted shortening or corn oil
¾ cup milk or water
butter or bacon fat

At home, measure dry ingredients into medium mixing bowl; mix well. Add melted shortening, and work with a spoon until mixture is fine and crumbly. Seal in a large, sturdy, plastic bag, ready for the back pack. At the campsite, when you are ready to make the bannock, open the bag; stir the ingredients to form a well for the water; gradually stir in the water, and work mixture into a stiff dough. You may need to use a little less or a little more water for a dough stiff enough to hold its shape. On floured foil place on a flat-top rock, and working with lightly floured hands, pat the dough into a flat cake the size of the griddle. Grease griddle lightly; heat it; set bread on it;

Figures A through E show how wire coat hangers can be used to improvise a number of cooking tools and pans for the camper. To be effective, the tools must be made from very stiff wire. Work with gloved hands, and use pliers to bend, shape, and twist the wire. Twisting the wires reinforces the handles. A wire cutter makes cutting the hangers easy.

1: Stirring premixed dry ingredients for trail bread. If the plastic bag is strong, liquids can be added and mixed in bag.

2: The bread is shaped to fit the pan on well-floured foil spread on a rock. Handle dough gently with floured hands.

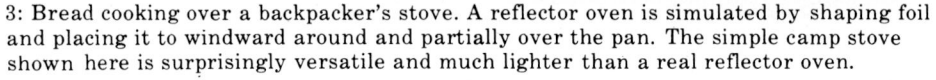

3: Bread cooking over a backpacker's stove. A reflector oven is simulated by shaping foil and placing it to windward around and partially over the pan. The simple camp stove shown here is surprisingly versatile and much lighter than a real reflector oven.

protect to windward with foil (see photograph 3). Cook 10 minutes on one side; flip with a spatula, and cook 10 minutes on the other side. Makes 4 to 6 servings.

### Corn Pone

1 cup yellow corn meal
1 cup sifted all-purpose flour
¼ cup sugar
4 teaspoons baking powder
1 teaspoon salt
½ cup powdered milk

3 teaspoons powdered egg (or 1 fresh egg, if available)
1 cup water
¼ cup melted bacon fat or butter, or ¼ cup salad oil

At home, measure dry ingredients into a mixing bowl; include powdered egg unless you will have fresh eggs at the campsite. Seal in a large, sturdy, plastic bag, ready for back packing. It will keep indefinitely. At the campsite, mix ingredients in the bag slightly (corn meal tends to settle to the bottom of the bag). Add the egg if you are using a fresh one. Then add the water and half the bacon fat, and mix thoroughly in the bag to make a semiliquid dough. Heat the remaining bacon fat in the griddle; pour in corn-pone dough, and cook until the top of the batter is as dry as a pancake ready to flip—about 10 minutes. Flip the corn cake, and cook another 10 minutes. Makes 6 servings.

If you want to try the Sourdough French Bread described on the next page as a camp treat, cook it in biscuit-size lumps on a griddle just as the cornpone and bannock doughs are baked. Cook the biscuits about 2 minutes more per side to compensate for cooler outdoor air and uncertain heat.

# Sourdough bread

The miners of the 1849 gold rush in California were called sourdoughs because the smell of the souring starter used to raise their camp bread followed them from site to site. The starter, then as now, is a mixture of water, flour, and yeast. After it has stood for three days, it gives off a strong, sour smell. In making sourdough for bread, a cupful of the starter is mixed with ¼ teaspoon baking soda; this alkali, with the acid dough, creates a powerful leavening agent, and this is added to the bread ingredients, as yeast would be added.

Sourdough bread has the starter's characteristic strong odor and, when an older starter is used, the wonderful flavor of sour-rye bread. Some starters sold commercially are said to be as much as 100 years old. (The longest I've kept one alive is 2½ years.) Made with very young starter, according to the recipes on the following pages, bread, biscuits and hot cakes have the sweet flavor of yeast-raised bread.

If you use your starter daily, the crock can stand in a cool spot in the kitchen. If you use it weekends, as I do, refrigerate it during the week. If you use it only occasionally, keep it frozen, and thaw 48 hours before using. The night before you are ready to bake, set the starter in a warm spot, and add 1½ cups of warm water and 2 cups of flour to it. In the morning, it should be bubbling merrily. You can reactivate a fading

*Craftsman John McGrath, who lives in New Jersey, has five children and is an enthusiastic gardener, beekeeper, and collector of Americana. He also is a great weekend chef. His sourdough recipes were developed in the course of dozens of Saturday-afternoon baking sessions.*

The finished loaves are crusty on the outside, tender and pungent inside. Sourdough is delicious with butter or jam, excellent with cheese fondue.

◄ The sourdough loaves, tops slashed, are put in a preheated oven two loaves at a time. Baking sheet is dusted with corn meal to prevent sticking.

starter by adding ½ package of dry yeast. Never add anything but flour and water to the starter. I do not use a soda activator for bread; though purists still do.

With age, the starter does settle and a liquid will float on top. If this liquid shades toward orange, discard it and start all over again.

The recipes on the following pages are made with the starter recipe below. You'll see that lots of good things can be made with sourdough.

### Sourdough Starter

In room-temperature container, dissolve ½ teaspoon dry yeast in 1½ cups warm water. Sift together 2 cups all-purpose flour, 1 teaspoon salt, and 3 tablespoons sugar; stir into yeast mixture. Cover; keep in warm place three days; stir twice daily. Starter is ready when it is thick, white, and bubbly.

### John's Sourdough French Bread

½ cup reconstituted evaporated milk
2 tablespoons shortening or margarine
1 tablespoon sugar
2 teaspoons salt
1½ cups sourdough starter

2½ to 3½ cups unsifted
   all-purpose flour
1 teaspoon vegetable oil
Corn meal

In small saucepan over low heat, stir milk and shortening until shortening is melted. Add sugar and salt, stir until dissolved. Combine slightly cooled milk mixture and starter in a large bowl. Stir in 2½ cups flour. When dough is mixed, turn it onto floured board, and knead 7 to 10 minutes, until dough is smooth and elastic. Add more flour if needed to keep dough from becoming sticky. Place in bowl greased with vegetable oil, turn dough greased side up. Cover bowl with plastic wrap to prevent crusting; let rise in warm place (85F) until double in bulk, 2 to 3 hours. Punch down; knead in ½ cup flour. Let rise again, until double, then punch down again. Divide in half; flatten, and shape into two 12-inch loaves (pages 288 and 289). Set loaves on a greased baking sheet sprinkled with corn meal. Cover, and let rise until doubled in size. Preheat oven to 400F. Brush loaves with water; make four diagonal slashes in tops. Set a pan of hot water on the oven's lower shelf. Heat an iron (or brick) to sizzling hot and insert it into the pan. The steam it creates will make a crisp crust. Remove the pan after the first 10 minutes of baking. Bake loaves 25 to 30 minutes, until browned. Cool on racks. Makes 2 loaves.

Small ceramic jar with a lid is John McGrath's preferred container for making sourdough starter. Miners of 1849 and today's campers make and carry starter in a small pail. Friction-top lid makes the best seal if pail is to be carried around.

To avoid overheating milk, John sets shortening in pot with premeasured milk, sugar and salt nearby, ready to be added as soon as shortening has melted.

## Sourdough Pizza Crust

| | |
|---|---|
| 1 cup sourdough starter | 1 tablespoon melted butter |
| 1 teaspoon salt | 1 cup flour |

Mix first three ingredients. Work in enough flour to make a dough that can be rolled into a thin layer. Put it on an oiled baking sheet, and bake in a preheated 500F oven about 5 minutes. Spread baked dough with your favorite pizza sauce and trimmings, such as the traditional cheese or other variations including sausage, anchovies, mushrooms. Bake at 425F until sauce bubbles, about 15 minutes.

4: Mixing flour into the starter-milk mixture. Work the dough until ingredients are thoroughly combined. When ready, it will be stiff and will look like this.

5: Kneading the dough on a floured board. After it has been kneaded for about 10 minutes, it will become smooth and elastic, and will be ready for raising.

Crusty and delicious French Sourdough loaves would make any meal a feast.

6: Dough is then placed in a large bowl greased with vegetable oil. Roll dough around in the bowl until shiny with oil, then turn greasiest side up for raising.

7: Cover the bowl with a sheet of plastic wrap, or with a very damp, clean towel. Set it in a warm spot to raise. Avoid places where drafts can get at it.

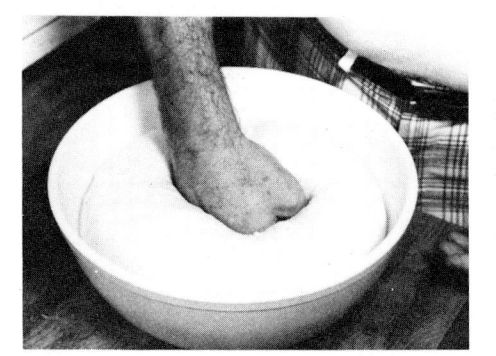

8: Dough will look like this when it has completely risen. Punch it down to remove air bubbles. Treat it quite roughly. Your aim is to really flatten it.

9: The dough looks like this when nearly all the air bubbles have been punched out of it. It will retain the impression of your fist.

10: To knead dough, fold over on itself and heel in the sides with your palms; move the dough clockwise on a floured board as you work.

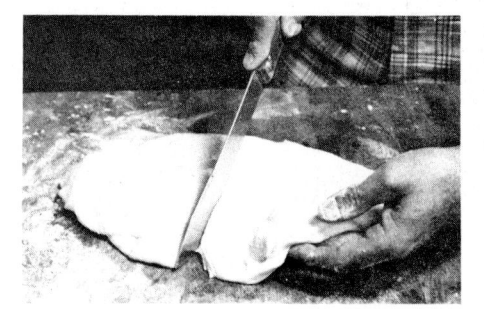

11: Halve the flattened dough with a sharp knife dipped in hot water.

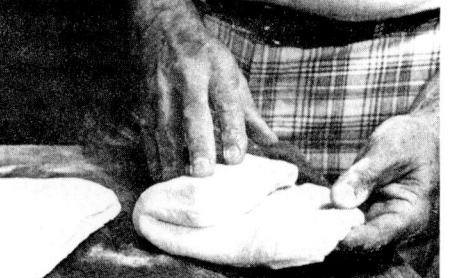

12: Fold sides of the dough in toward the center, as though making an envelope.

13: Flatten the dough into a rectangle, and press out any air bubbles.

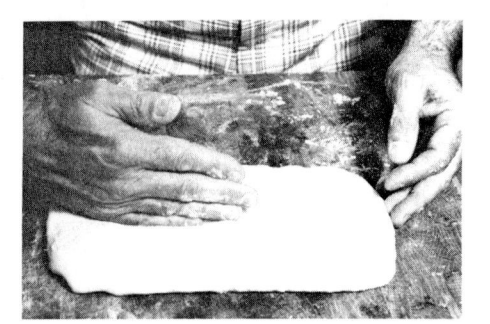

14: Crease dough down the center with the heel of your hand, and fold it over.

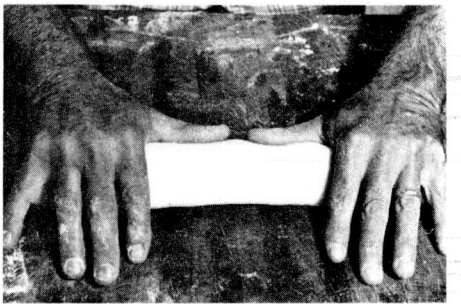

15: Roll into a loaf about 12 inches long, shaping it as you roll.

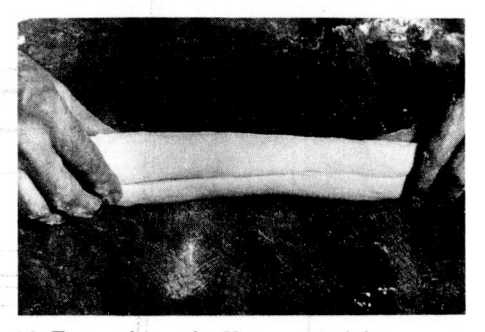

16: Taper the ends. Keep a straight seam down the underside of the loaf.

**Other McGrath Family Favorites**
Sourdough Biscuits and Sourdough Hotcakes and Sourdough Applesauce Cake are only a few of the many other bakery products that can be made using the Sourdough Starter as the leavening agent. Almost any recipe calling for yeast, and in which a bready, slightly sour flavor is desirable, can be made with Sourdough Starter.

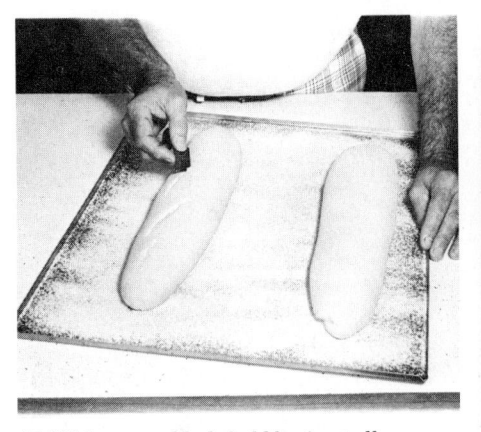

17: With a razor blade held horizontally, make three or four slits in each loaf. Make cuts shallow, so the dough will not fall.

▶ 18: Steam is the secret of crusty loaves. John plunges a sizzling hot antique flatiron into pan of hot water to make steam the first 10 minutes of baking.

## Sourdough Biscuits

2 cups sifted all-purpose flour
2 teaspoons baking powder
1 tablespoon sugar
½ teaspoon salt
½ cup butter
2 cups sourdough starter

Mix dry ingredients. Cut in butter until mixture looks like bread crumbs. Stir in starter. Turn dough onto floured board; knead lightly; work in more flour if dough is sticky. Roll out ½ inch thick. Cut in 2½-inch-diameter circles. Place on oiled baking sheet, and let rise ½ hour. Bake in preheated 425F oven 20 to 25 minutes, until browned. Makes 20 to 22 biscuits.

## McGrath's Sourdough Hot Cakes

1 cup sourdough starter
2 teaspoons salt
1/3 cup melted butter
¼ cup dry skim milk
1 teaspoon baking soda, dissolved in a little water
2 tablespoons sugar
2 eggs

In a large bowl mix all ingredients thoroughly. Pour ¼ cupful at a time, onto a medium hot griddle, lightly greased. When the top becomes dry looking, in 3 or 4 minutes, turn and cook another 3 minutes or until second side is golden brown. Makes 4 to 6 servings.

## Sourdough Applesauce Cake

1 cup sourdough starter
¼ cup dry skim milk
1 cup applesauce
½ cup granulated sugar
½ cup brown sugar
½ cup butter
1 egg, well beaten
1 cup applesauce
1 cup sifted, all-purpose flour
½ teaspoon salt
½ teaspoon nutmeg
½ teaspoon allspice
1 teaspoon cinnamon
½ teaspoon ground cloves
2 teaspoons baking soda

19: When the loaves sound hollow when thumped, they are done. If they are not ready, put them back for 5 minutes.

Mix sourdough starter, milk and applesauce, and set aside in a warm place. Cream together the sugars and butter; stir in egg and remaining ingredients. Add sourdough mixture, and beat only enough to blend it in. Put in an 8-by-8 inch cake pan and bake in preheated 350F oven 50 minutes. Cool, then turn out on a cake rack. For related entries, see "Bread Sculpture," "Cheeses and Churning," "Gingerbread," "Marmalades and Preserves."

# BREAD SCULPTURE
## Offbeat Art Form

*Barbara Auran-Wrenn is an interior and craft designer specializing in contemporary folk art, including assemblages, soft stuffed sculpture, and bread sculpture. Barbara also does illustrations for magazines, has been a display director, and has taught art to children.*

Bread sculpture, the baking of bread in fanciful shapes, has its origins in ancient rituals. The Egyptians molded their bread into primitive birds and flowers and offered them to their gods. Bread was sacred to the Greeks and Romans, and there are numerous references to it in the Bible. The early Coptic Christians imprinted their ritual loaves with clay seals.

Bread sculpture as we know it today probably had its origins in medieval times in Europe. The Scandinavians, drawing on their Viking heritage, shaped their bread into suns and mythical animals. In Central Europe and the Balkans, bread played a major role in holiday celebrations and in Germany bread bakers tried to outdo each other in creating elaborate bread sculptures.

Some of the shapes have survived. In some parts of Italy, during the Easter holidays, walls, tables and bakeries are decorated with many-bosomed bread ladies, descendants of the statues of fertility goddesses that were common in Rome and Greece during the pre-Christian era.

These bread sculptures, based on traditional folk-art designs, can be made as holiday treats or varnished and hung on the wall.

Although now adapted to twentieth century needs, bread sculpturing retains some of the magic of ancient ritual. There is great suspense as the bread rises, puffs into the desired shape, and then browns into permanence. Few other crafts do as much to create an atmosphere of celebration.

To get started in bread sculpture, work with the shapes on these pages. When you have mastered the process, develop your own sculptures. Use the Bread Sculpture Dough, page 291, for breads to be eaten. Use the Bread Clay recipe for shapes, like the mirror on page 291, for permanent display.

## Bread sculpture dough (edible)

2½ cups warm water (105-115F);
2 packages dry yeast;
1 tablespoon salt;
1 tablespoon melted butter;
7 cups flour;
1 egg white mixed with 1 tablespoon
water for glaze

Measure water into large mixing bowl.
Sprinkle yeast over water; stir to
dissolve. Add salt and melted butter.
Add flour; mix well. Do not allow
dough to rise. If dough is sticky,
add more flour when rolling out.
Pull off enough dough to work with;
refrigerate balance.

Materials for sculpture: Scissors,
wax paper, orange stick or dull
knife, bay leaf, peppercorns, food
coloring, saucers, No. 4 water color
paint brush, cookie sheet.

Enlarge pattern according to
directions on page 57 of Volume One.
Trace pattern onto wax paper using
orange stick to make an imprint.
Roll out dough to ⅜-inch thickness.
Lay pattern on dough; trace, bearing
down to make an impression on dough.
Cut around impression with scissors;
stretch dough to make sun rays and
bird's tail.

Refer to illustrations for final
shapes, but use your imagination for
bending shapes into free form design.

Coloring: Place several drops of
food coloring in a saucer, using
separate saucer for each color.
Colors can be mixed. Yellow added
to green makes a strong spring green;
blue added sparingly to red makes
purple. Dilute with one tablespoon
water. Brush onto dough with swift
strokes. Do not soak. Rinse out
brush under running water before
using next color. Colors may run
into each other on dough which
creates pleasing effect.

Bake sculpture in 450F oven for
10 minutes, or until just beginning
to brown. Five minutes before it's
done, glaze with egg white and
water mixture, using pastry brush
to apply, to give bread hard, glossy
surface. Bake 5 minutes more. Remove
from oven. Place on rack to cool.

(If the sculpture is to be hung,
insert a paper clip or bent wire in
the top of the shape before baking.)

Baker's clay makes a sculptured frame
for a mirror. Baker's clay can be shaped
by hand, rolled flat, or cut with cookie
cutters. Textures can be indented with
cookie cutters. Textures can be indented
with a variety of objects.

## Bread Sculpture Mirror

The mirror framed in bread sculpture,
above, is made with a three-inch oval
mirror imbedded in Baker's Clay, the
dough used for display sculptures.

## Baker's Clay (not edible)

**Materials:** 1-pound package of baking
soda, 1 cup cornstarch, 1¼ cups
cold water, rolling pin, cardboard
(5 x 8½ inches), food coloring,
wax paper, No. 4 watercolor paint
brush, sharp knife, white glue, pencil.

Combine baking soda and cornstarch
in saucepan. Add water. Mix with fork
until smooth. Cook 1 minute over
medium heat. Spoon onto plate.
Cover with damp cloth; allow to cool.

Cut cardboard into shape 5 x 8½
inches with rounded top, as indicated
by pattern. Trace pattern on rolled-
out clay as directed above. Cut out
with sharp knife, keeping excess
clay damp. Assemble pieces and
lay on cardboard backing. Imbed
mirror in center of lower half
while clay is soft. Dry for 24
hours, glue together. Paint with
food coloring.

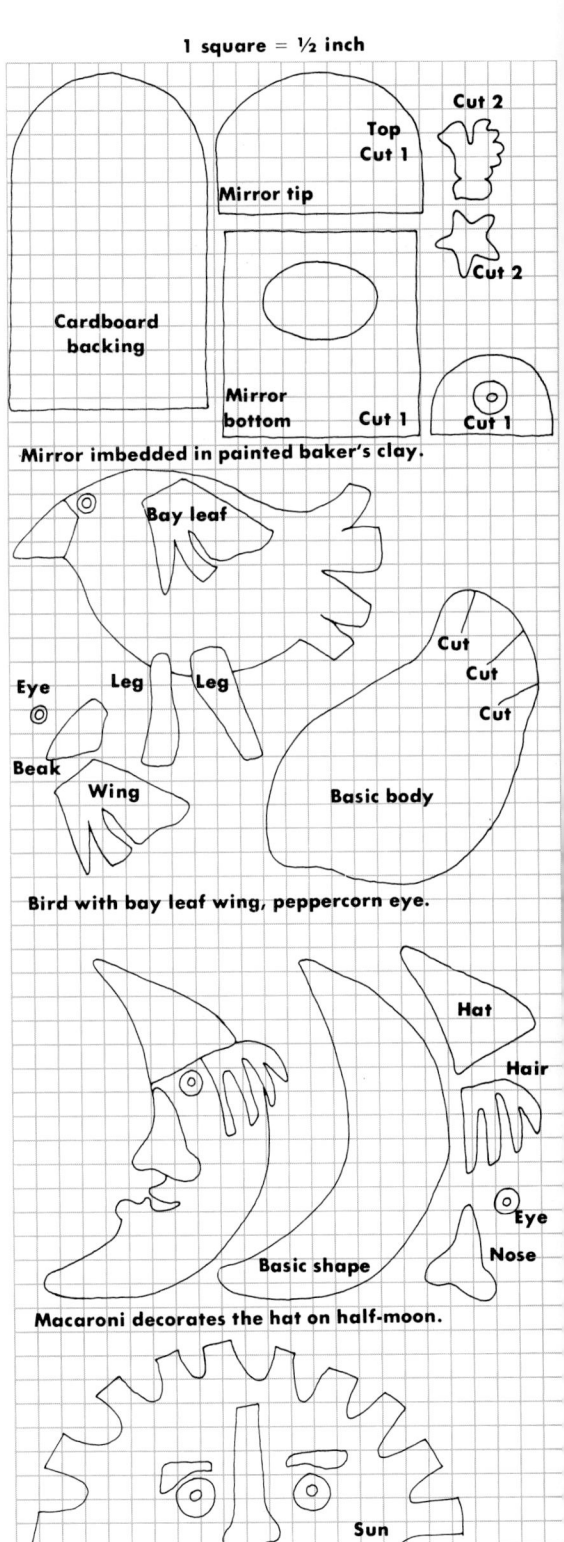

1 square = ½ inch

Mirror imbedded in painted baker's clay.

Bird with bay leaf wing, peppercorn eye.

Macaroni decorates the hat on half-moon.

The sun's rays are stretched dough.

# BREWING
# With Roots and Herbs

*Nicholas E. Leddo has been making wines and beers, alcoholic and nonalcoholic, for 15 years. He has conducted a television series on winemaking and has lectured extensively on brewing.*

From Colonial times until quite recently, the brewing of soft drinks and ales was a popular domestic art in America. Of the two types of brew, beer was the more important to the Colonists. In fact, it was a factor in the *Mayflower's* landing at Plymouth instead of Virginia. A 1622 manuscript records the decision made during the historic voyage of 1620: "for we could not now take time for further search or consideration, our victuals being spent, especially our beer." The first commercial brewery in America was built a year later in lower Manhattan by the Dutch West India Company.

Early commercial breweries were like the one shown on this page, where horses, plodding around a capstan in the brewery basement (see inset at right) provided the motive force for grinding grain, usually barley, which makes the malt used in beer recipes. A series of cogwheels (F and G) powered by the capstan in the basement turns the grindstone (H). Grain arrives from the

granary on an upper floor through the pipe (K), while the ground meal is
bagged (I) and taken to the brewing kettles. The commercial breweries were
few, so farmers and innkeepers made their own beers as well as soft drinks.

The first recipes used by home brewers were brought from Europe; but over
the years the American home brewer developed some beers—light, carbonated
beverages with a tang to them—that were nonalcoholic and particularly
American. Root beer, sarsaparilla, and spruce beers are among them. Produced
in home kitchens and relying often on roots and barks found locally, these
drinks were the basis for the soft-drink industry which flourishes today.

At the present time, federal law prohibits the home brewing of beers made
of fermented hops and malt. You cannot get a license to make your own brew
as you can to make your own wine, but no law prohibits making the old-time
soft beers. Recipes for many of these are given on the following pages.

1: Equipment useful in making soft drinks includes 10-gallon plastic pail; 5-gallon carboy; 5-foot siphon hose; wooden spoon; 2-ounce packet of chlorine detergent; nylon straining bag. To bottle carbonated beverages you will need: bottle filler; bottle capper; crown bottle caps and 12-ounce bottles.

## Kitchen Favorites and Celebrations
# Root beer and sarsaparilla

The beverages below are generally known as soft drinks, but they are not the carbonated drinks you buy ready-bottled at the grocery store. They are naturally fermented brews carbonated by the action of yeast and sugar or other fizzmaking ingredients, such as cream of tartar. They contain a small amount of alcohol, usually less than one-half of one percent, and may be brewed legally without purchase of a license.

Much of the equipment used for making these drinks you may already have in your kitchen, especially if you make your own jams and jellies and have five-gallon kettles for the purpose. The equipment used for making carbonated drinks appears in photograph 1. Indispensable items for carbonated beverages are the bottles made specifically for carbonated beverages, bottle filler, bottle capper and crown bottle caps.

Caution: Bottle carbonated brews only in new bottles purchased for the purpose. Throw away bottles that have held carbonated beverages from the store may not be strong enough to withstand the gas pressure that builds up in some homemade brews and could burst.

On these pages there are old-fashioned recipes for beverages that are not carbonated and therefore do not require a bottle capper. Try those first to see if making soft drinks and brews is an activity your family enjoys.

Equipment that you can't find locally can usually be purchased from firms that sell brewing supplies, such as Specialty Products International,

Root beer is a favorite soft drink of young and old alike. This brew, homemade, has more body and flavor than commercial drinks.

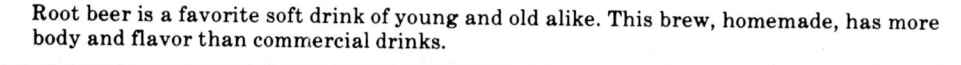

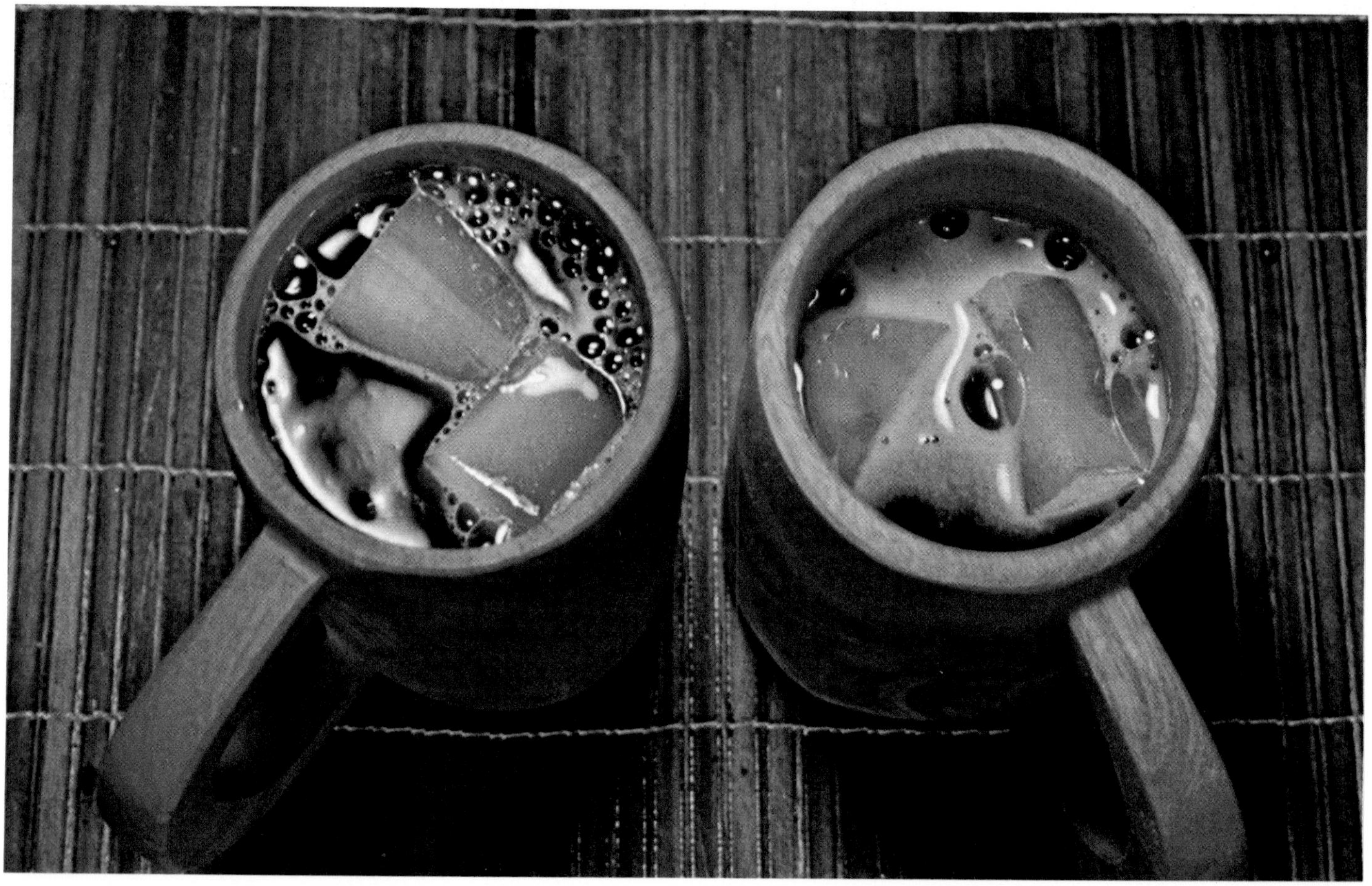

Ltd., Box 784, Chapel Hill, N.C. 27514, and Wine Art Shop, 1109 Front Street, Uniondale, N.Y. 11553.

Before you make your own brew, sterilize the equipment to be used, the containers, the tubes, and the bottles—even if they are new. The easiest way to sterilize is to wash everything thoroughly with a chlorinated-detergent solution. If the local hardware shops don't carry chlorine detergent suitable for this purpose, buy from a brewing-supply house. Mix two ounces of the detergent with one gallon of warm water, and wash everything in this solution. Be sure to rinse away all traces of the chlorine after the detergent has been used. Any solution left in the bottles or on the equipment might affect brews that include yeast and could spoil the flavor of others.

### Root Beer

Homemade root beer is flavored with an extract made from the root of the sarsaparilla plant, a trailing tropical vine, of the *Smilax* genus, that grows in America. The recipe below is typical of soft-drink recipes of home brews.

### Root Beer

4 pounds granulated sugar
4¾ gallons lukewarm water
3 ounces root-beer extract

½ teaspoon dry baker's yeast
1 cup lukewarm water

Place the sugar in a 10-gallon plastic pail, and pour in the root-beer extract. Mix well, to distribute the extract as evenly as possible through the sugar granules. Mix the yeast in the cup of lukewarm water, and let it stand

2: Pour the root-beer extract from the bottle right onto the sugar. Mix thoroughly so the extract is distributed evenly through the sugar.

3: Making the yeast mixture. Sprinkle over the cup of warm water; stir, and let stand. Be sure to use the exact amount of yeast specified in the recipe.

4: Adding water to sugar-and-extract mixture. Pour the water slowly to avoid splashing. Pouring and mixing are easy in a 10-gallon plastic pail.

for 5 minutes. (Do not use more yeast than the recipe specifies; if you do, the drink will be unpalatable and excessive gas pressure may develop in the bottles.) Pour 4¾ gallons of lukewarm water from the tap into the pail to dissolve the sugar. (If stronger flavor is desired, reduce the sugar to 3½ pounds and the water to 4 gallons.) Add the yeast mixture to the sugar mixture (see photograph 5), and blend well. The next step is to siphon the beer into a 5-gallon carboy. Let the mixture rest for an hour so that any sediment (which might affect the beer's flavor) will settle. Then, using the siphon hose or a bottle filler, fill 12-ounce carbonated-beverage bottles to within ½ inch of the top; more air space might cause spoilage. Seal the bottles with a hand capping machine and crown bottle caps (photograph 7).

Keep the bottles on their sides in a warm place away from drafts until you see bubbles forming. Root beer should be ready to drink about 5 days after bottling (longer in cool weather). After 5 days, place a bottle in the refrigerator; chill well, and taste the root beer. If the carbonation is adequate, put the other bottles in a cool place with an even temperature. Just before serving, refrigerate for a short time to make the root beer really cold and to prevent excess foaming. When home-brewed beer is served, fill the glasses or the pitcher in one pouring to avoid stirring up sediment.

Makes about 5 gallons, or about 50 (12-ounce) bottles.

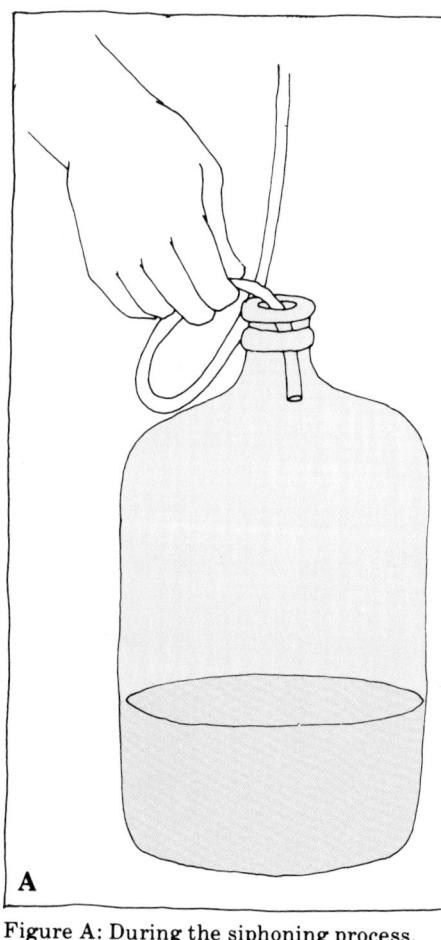

Figure A: During the siphoning process, the exit end of the hose is held high so the beer will be aerated as it splashes into the carboy. Carboy is placed well below the pail so that all liquid is siphoned off, leaving behind as much sediment as possible.

5: Adding the yeast mixture to the sugar mixture. Empty the cup. Then, to make sure all the yeast is added, dip up a cupful of the sugar mixture, swirl it around the cup and dump back into pail.

6: Bottle filler, attached to siphon at other end, is inserted. Lower filler tip to within ½ inch of bottle bottom. You can fill bottles with the siphon end alone, but a filler makes the job easier.

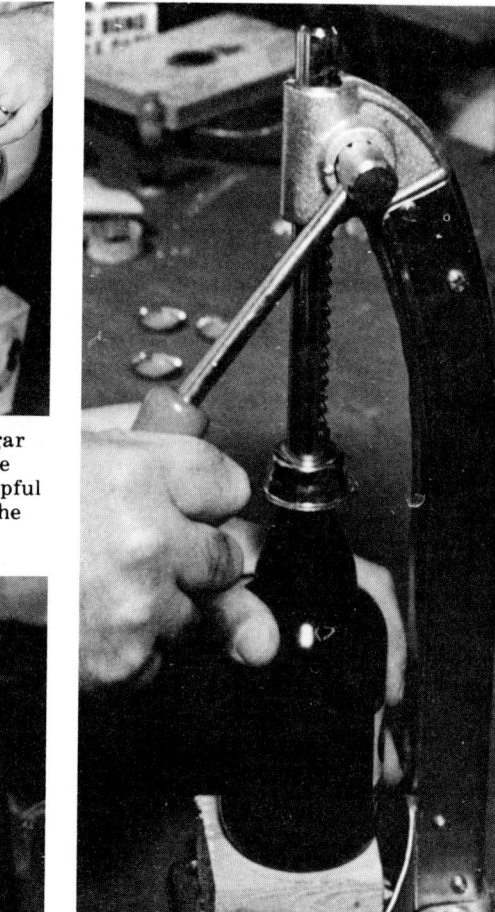

7: Using a hand-operated crown capper. Place the bottle on a block, if necessary, to get it high enough to receive the cap at maximum pressure. Center each cap before pressing down the capping lever.

## Other Sarsaparilla Drinks

Commercial root beer is made from a liquid extract of sarsaparilla combined with wintergreen and other flavoring agents. Sarsaparillas were very popular in the late nineteenth and early twentieth centuries, when it was generally believed that sarsaparilla was a tonic and could cure a long list of ailments. So fervent was the belief in its curative powers that many elixirs touted by traveling salesmen were flavored with it, and almost every homemaker had a recipe for making her own sarsaparilla brew. Today, faith in sarsaparilla's medicinal value has vanished, but it still is used to mask the flavor of unpleasant medicines, and it still makes a pleasant, light drink similar to those made in homes long ago.

Compare the modern recipes for Sarsaparilla and Sarsaparilla Syrup below with the recipe for Sarsaparilla Mead, which is more than 100 years old. It appears in a recipe book titled *The Young Homemaker's Friend*, which was written by a Mrs. Cornelius and was published in Boston in 1859 by Brown, Taggard and Chase. Mead is a name usually applied to drinks in which honey is the main sweetener, but the term is also used for many light drinks flavored with sugar rather than honey.

## Old-time Sarsaparilla Mead

"Three pounds of sugar, three ounces of tartaric acid, one ounce of cream of tartar, one of flour, one of essence of sarsaparilla, and 3 quarts of water. Strain and bottle it, then let it stand ten days before using it."

The modern version relies on sugar and yeast to start its bubbles going and omits the cream of tartar, tartaric acid, and flour. Although a nylon strainer is called for in the recipe, a clean nylon stocking will do the job as well. Sterilize your equipment as described above, and bottle the drink in 12-ounce bottles intended for carbonated beverages.

## Sarsaparilla

9 cups sugar
5 gallons lukewarm water
2 ounces sarsaparilla extract

½ teaspoon dry baker's yeast
1 cup lukewarm water

Dissolve sugar in the 5 gallons of lukewarm water in a 6- or 10-gallon container. Add sarsaparilla extract, and stir thoroughly. Mix the yeast in the cup of lukewarm water until dissolved. Strain through a nylon strainer into the sugar mixture, and stir well. Transfer into sterilized bottles, using the bottle filler or the siphon, as described in the recipe for Root Beer, page 295. Store in a warm place for 5 days. Chill before serving.

Makes 5 gallons, or about 50 12-ounce bottles.

Sarsaparilla made this way is naturally fermented and refreshingly fizzy. You can also make an excellent sarsaparilla drink with Sarsaparilla Syrup, below. Just mix the syrup with sparkling club soda.

## Sarsaparilla Syrup

7 cups sugar
4½ cups hot water

2 ounces sarsaparilla extract

Pour the sugar into the hot water in a 3-quart kettle or a plastic container. Add extract, and mix well. As soon as the sugar is completely dissolved, the syrup is ready to use. To flavor an 8-ounce glass of club soda, add 2 or 3 tablespoons of syrup. Makes enough to flavor 40 to 50 8-ounce drinks.

Sarsaparilla is only one of the many root and bark flavorings used to make soft drinks. The early recipes given on pages 298 to 301 are similar to the modern versions that follow them. Some of the ingredients in the early versions—pine buds, for instance—are hard to find, but many of them can be purchased from herb stores and mail-order supply houses such as Caswell-Massey Co. Ltd., 320 West 13th Street, New York, N.Y. 10014.

Reproduction of an old soft-drink poster advertising root beer in the early days of commercial soft drinks, when many people on homesteads and farms were still brewing their own cooling potions.

## Kitchen Favorites and Celebrations
# Ginger beer, other delights

Another old-time favorite is ginger beer, translated by the soft-drink industry into ginger ale. It is interesting to compare the three following recipes. The Nineteenth-Century English Ginger Beer uses brown sugar and lemons, with ginger and cream of tartar and yeast for flavor and fizz. The two modern recipes rely on ginger and yeast, but resemble the 1859 version.

In preparing the brews in this section, follow the same general procedures described for Root Beer, page 295. The equipment is essentially the same—hose and bottle filler for siphoning (to avoid transferring sediment to bottles), large plastic pail for the mixing. The bottle capper, bottles, and crown caps will be needed for beverages that will be carbonated. Sterilize the equipment before using it, as instructed on page 295.

Drinks that have yeast as an ingredient generally taste better if they are allowed to rest several days before they are served, so the flavor can ripen and the sediment settle. Those without yeast usually can be served at once. In these recipes, as in those with sarsaparilla root, the water is lukewarm to dissolve the sugar easily. But if you are planning to mix the ingredients in a crock or a large, heavy container instead of a plastic pail, it is a good idea to warm the crock or container first by scalding it with a kettleful of boiling water, as suggested in the recipe for Yankee Switchel, page 300.

### Nineteenth-Century English Ginger Beer
"Pour four quarts of boiling water, upon an ounce and a half of ginger, an ounce of cream of tartar, a pound of clean brown sugar, and two fresh lemons sliced thin. It should be wrought twenty-four hours, with two gills (½ pint) of good yeast, and then bottled. It improves by keeping several weeks, unless the weather is hot, and it is an excellent beverage. If made with loaf instead of brown sugar, the appearance and flavor are finer."

### Modern Ginger Beer I

| | |
|---|---|
| 2 cups sugar | 1 cup warm water |
| 2 lemons | 1 tablespoon cream of tartar |
| 6 quarts warm water | 2 tablespoons ground ginger |
| ¼ teaspoon dry baker's yeast | |

Mix sugar and juice of the lemons in a large bowl. Pour in 6 quarts warm water, and stir well to dissolve sugar. Let stand until tepid. While mixture is cooling, dissolve yeast in 1 cup warm water, and add to cream of tartar and ginger. Add this to sugar mixture, and stir thoroughly. Pour into 12-ounce bottles for carbonated beverages, and seal with crown caps. Lay bottles on their sides in a cool place 5 days. Beer is then ready to serve. Makes 16 (12-ounce) bottles.

### Modern Ginger Beer II

| | |
|---|---|
| 1 ounce fresh ginger root | 1 gallon rapidly boiling water |
| 1 pound loaf sugar | ½ ounce yeast cake |
| ½ ounce cream of tartar | 2 teaspoons granulated sugar |
| 2 lemons | |

In a small mortar or on a wooden cutting board, bruise the ginger root. Put it in a 4-quart bowl or kettle with loaf sugar and cream of tartar. With a potato peeler, peel rind from lemon as thinly as possible. Remove white pith with a sharp knife. Slice lemon thinly. Add lemon peel and slices to ginger mixture. Pour boiling water into the bowl; stir with a wooden spoon. Let

The popularity of brewing in medieval times is reflected in this period woodcut of a reveler with a glass of beer.

Homemade ginger beer occasionally develops quite a head and has a sharp, tangy flavor. It is flavored with either fresh or ground ginger.

cool to lukewarm. Cream yeast with granulated sugar, and add to the mixture. Cover bowl with foil, and leave it for a day in a moderately warm room. Then strain liquid through a nylon strainer. Bottle and cap as in preceding recipe. Let rest 4 days. Chill before serving.

Makes 10 (12-ounce) bottles.

A variation of ginger beer is Switchel, an old-time Yankee thirst quencher.

### Yankee Switchel

2 gallons warm water
4 cups sugar
2 cups molasses

2 cups good cider vinegar
2 teaspoons ground ginger

Scald a 4-gallon crock or kettle with a kettleful of boiling water. Pour in the warm water. Stir in sugar and molasses, mixing until sugar has completely dissolved. Stir in vinegar and ginger, and mix well. Let cool. Bottle in 2 sterilized gallon jugs. Store in refrigerator.

Makes 2 gallons.

### Other Types of Root-Flavored Beer

The recipe for Nineteenth-Century Spring Beer, the most complex of the three early recipes given below, calls for wintergreen, pine buds, molasses, yeast, and hops. The recipe for Spruce and Boneset Beer also relies on hops for flavor. Boneset, *Eupatorium perfoliatum*, is a North American herb once believed to be helpful in the setting of bones.

### Nineteenth Century Spring Beer

"Take a handful of checkerberry (wintergreen), a few sassafras roots cut up, a half handful of pine-buds, while they are small and gummy, and a small handful of hops. (If dried in the ordinary way. But a small pinch of hops put up in pound packages by the Shakers is enough.) Put all these into a pail of water over night, and in the morning boil them two or three hours; fill up the kettle when it boils away. Strain it into a jar or firkin (¼ barrel) that will hold half a pailful more of water. Stir in a pint and a half of molasses, then add the half pailful of water, and taste it. If not sweet enough add more molasses. It loses the sweetness a little in the process of fermentation, and should therefore be made rather too sweet at first. Add two or three gills (½ or ¾ pint) of good yeast, set it in a warm place, and let it remain undisturbed till it is fermented. When the top is covered with a thick, dark foam, take it off; have ready clean bottles and good corks; pour off the beer into another vessel, so gently as not to disturb the sediment; then bottle it, and set it in a cool place. It will be ready for use in two days. The sediment should be put into a bottle by itself, loosely corked, and kept to ferment the next brewing."

A current recipe for Modern Spring Beer follows much the same procedure and is made with similar ingredients.

### Modern Spring Beer

4 pounds brown sugar
2 cups dark molasses
3 quarts boiling water
1 ounce essence of sassafras

4 ounces cream of tartar
1 ounce essence of checkerberry (wintergreen)

In a 1-gallon crock or kettle, mix sugar, molasses, and boiling water. Use the last bit of boiling water to rinse out the cup in which you measured the molasses. Stir until water becomes lukewarm. Then add cream of tartar. When cool, add checkerberry and sassafras; mix well. Store in a 1-gallon jug, capped, in the refrigerator. Use 2 tablespoons of this mixture to 8 ounces of cold water. To make a fizzy drink add ⅓ teaspoon baking soda to each glass.

Makes enough for about 150 (8-ounce) glasses.

## Modern Spruce Beer

2 quarts of boiling water
½ teaspoon oil of spruce
½ teaspoon oil of sassafras
½ teaspoon oil of wintergreen

2 gallons cold water
1½ pints dark molasses
1 cake yeast, crumbled

Pour the boiling water into a 5- or 10-gallon container. Stir in spruce, sassafras, and wintergreen; mix well. Stir in the cold water, molasses, and yeast. When yeast is completely dissolved, siphon mixture into a carboy; let rest 2 hours. Then bottle in 12-ounce bottles; cap. Let settle 48 hours before serving. Serve well chilled.

Makes 26 (12-ounce) bottles.

The following nineteenth-century recipe for various beers, from spruce to boneset, is similar, and is from Mrs. Cornelius' *Advice to Young Homemakers*.

## Early Recipe for Spruce and Boneset Beer

"Boil a small handful each of hops and boneset for an hour or two, in a pailful of water; strain it, and dilute it with cold water till it is of the right strength. Add a small tablespoon of essence of spruce, sweeten, ferment and bottle it, like spring beer.

"The essence of hops, checkerberry, ginger, and spruce, put into warm water in suitable proportions, then sweetened, fermented, and bottled, make good beer."

Spruce, with its tart, gummy taste, was an ingredient in many cooling drinks. There is no well-known modern equivalent for the Maple Beer recipe below, but once you have made some of the soft drinks described here, you may want to try your powers of interpretation on this set of ingredients. The unusual combination promises an interesting drink.

Brewer, circa 1600.

## Early Recipe for Maple Beer

"To four gallons of boiling water, add one quart of maple syrup and a small tablespoon of essence of spruce. When it is milk warm, add a pint of yeast; and when fermented bottle it. In three days it is fit for use."

## Kvass

Kvass, or quass, enjoys a traditional popularity among the peoples of Russia and eastern Europe. It is made by fermenting yeast and stale bread (usually rye) with the addition of sugar and sometimes fruit. With the following recipe, you can produce a drink with an exotic taste. The flavor of kvass isn't quite like that of any other drink.

## Kvass

2 pounds dark rye bread
8 quarts water
3 tablespoons dry baker's yeast,
  or 3 cakes yeast

1 quart warm water
⅔ cup honey
3 or 4 sprigs fresh mint

Slice bread thinly, and bake slices in oven at low temperature until they are crisp. Bring 8 quarts water to a boil in a large pot. Place rye rusks in the water, and let them soak 3 to 4 hours. Then strain liquid into another large pot. Dissolve yeast in 1 quart warm water. Add this to liquid from bread mixture. Then add honey. Crush mint, add, and stir thoroughly.

Place cheesecloth over the pot, anchoring it with string or tape. Put pot in a warm part of the room, and let the mixture ferment 6 hours. When froth appears, strain the kvass, and funnel it into 12-ounce size carbonated beverage bottles. Use the capper to seal with crown caps. Store in a cool place and let rest 6 days. Chill for several hours before serving.

Makes 21 (12-ounce) bottles.

For related projects, see the entry "Winemaking."

301

# BUTTONS
## Collect and Transform

*Viviane Beck Ertell of Solano Beach, Cal. is one of the country's best-known button collectors. Her notable collection of eighteenth and early nineteenth-century buttons is on display at The Viviane Beck Ertell Button Museum in Flemington, N.J. Mrs. Ertell's favorite museum pieces are featured and described in her profusely illustrated book,* The Colorful World of Buttons.

Few of us take much notice of the kind of buttons that are on our garments. We regard them as utilitarian and, at best, quietly decorative. However, buttons can be fascinating; you can turn them into jewelry, or learn how to make them out of found articles or suitable raw materials. And once you become aware of the variety and beauty of old buttons, you may find yourself—as have many others—beginning a collection.

In past centuries buttons were treasured costume accessories. All the techniques used in fine art—carving, painting, enameling, engraving—went into the making of beautiful buttons. Artisans designed buttons using precious metals and semiprecious stones. Collectors call such buttons "art in miniature." Although few buttons of high quality are now being made commercially, craftsmen are again producing handmade buttons for their own enjoyment.

We don't know when buttons first came into use. The earliest known button, unearthed in a Danish peat bog, is thought to have belonged to an Iron Age man. Old documents inform us that by the thirteenth century button makers had been organized into guilds, the medieval version of labor unions. Buttons were being made of precious metals and even Venetian glass in the fourteenth and fifteenth centuries—but very few of these early buttons have survived.

The extravagant Louis XIV of France made exquisite handworked buttons the rage. It is recorded that once when he was entertaining the Persian ambassador at dinner, the king was dressed in a costume with diamond buttons and diamond embroidery requiring twelve and a half thousand stones.

In the eighteenth century, button-making as an art reached its peak. Most of our oldest antique buttons date from this period. Every conceivable material and subject was used. Some famous artists, such as Fragonard and Isabey, painted miniatures for use in button-making. This was the age of the fop, and most fancy buttons were worn by men. Wealthy gentlemen would commission buttons picturing anything from hunting scenes to illustrations of Ovid's love poems.

When Queen Victoria's beloved Prince-Consort died, and she went into a long period of mourning, the English responded by wearing buttons of black glass. Some of these, called aristocrats, were decorated with gold and silver and are now rare finds.

After the War of 1812, foreign imports were limited, and American craftsmen began making the finely detailed gilt-brass Golden Age buttons.

Among modern buttons—those produced after World War I—one of the most interesting kinds is the paperweight, a decorated glass button that resembles a tiny desk paperweight.

### Button Collecting as a Hobby

There are many ways to start a button collection. Some people begin with a material they are already collecting, such as porcelain or Wedgwood. Buttons have been made from more than 200 materials. In the late 1800s, a patent was granted for blood buttons! Antique silver, enamel, and lithographs are popular among many collectors. Other people specialize in subject matter or historical periods.

Whatever your interests, the best way to start is with what you already have. I started my collection of eighteenth- and nineteenth-century buttons when my husband, an antiques dealer, acquired a collection he didn't want.

Lacy glass buttons from the late 1800s, when buttons were works of art rather than simple fasteners. (Viviane Beck Ertell Button Museum)

Rare 18th century buttons from Mrs. Ertell's collection: (top to bottom, left to right) bouquet of seed pearls on glass, classical figure in Wedgwood, memorial design in seed pearls, linen flowers on glass, horse of sulphide type, rustic scene carved in pearl, hunter painted on glass, insect of semiprecious stones on rock crystal, seated lady painted on ivory, balloon painted on paper, and country scene painted on ivory.

For you, it may be Grandmother's old button box. Our thrifty Colonial ancestors were great hoarders of buttons, which were passed down through the families to be used again and again. Or you may even come across one of the strings of buttons young ladies in the late 1800s were fond of making.

Before you begin searching for buttons, it may be helpful to read a book like my own, which explains and illustrates the many types of button. *The Collector's Encyclopedia of Buttons*, by Sally C. Luscomb, and *The Complete Button Book*, by Lillian Smith Albert, are also excellent references.

Where do you find collectable buttons? Surprisingly enough, you can often buy them in trimming shops and at notions counters of large department stores. There are also some specialty button boutiques, like Tender Buttons in New York City. Small antique shops may have boxes of old buttons tucked away in some dusty corner. Or you may come across some old pieces of clothing with interesting buttons on them.

If you are seriously interested in button collecting, write to the National Button Society. The publicity chairman is Mrs. Robert Montgomery, 3257 Silsby Road, Cleveland, Ohio 44118. This group of more than 2,000 collectors, formed in the early 1940s, can put you in touch with state and local button clubs. The bi-monthly national bulletin carries information about shows where buttons are exhibited, bought, and sold; and it lists the names and addresses of artisans who turn out beautiful handmade buttons. You can add to your collection by ordering these studio buttons directly from the craftsmen listed.

Whether you're a button collector or not, chances are you have a shoe box full of odd buttons. Some of these buttons may be quite beautiful. A few may even be antiques. They are probably singles or at most pairs, and you may think there isn't much you can do with them. But there is.

My button memorabilia has been a source of inspiration; I have turned some of my most beautiful buttons into jewelry, stringing them for necklaces and bracelets, or making them into earrings and cuff links.

Cuff links are a good beginning project for your button-jewelry collection. They are good-looking and easy to make. All you need are two favorite buttons (they don't have to be an exact match), a pair of cuff-link backs that you can buy at the sewing counter of most department stores, and a tube of household cement or any glue that adheres to metal. The buttons should have flat metal backs so they can be fitted smoothly to the cuff-link backs. They should also have small shanks that can be bent easily.

Try to remove the shanks with pliers. If this is not possible, flatten the shanks to the backs of the buttons. Usually, you can do this with your fingers. Next, spread a light coat of glue evenly over the back of one button and the round, flat surface of one cuff-link back. Press the cuff-link back against the button and hold for a minute or two. To test adhesion, lift the cuff link by the tip of the back. If the button doesn't hold, try pressing the button and the back of the link together for a longer time, or try another metal-bonding glue. Glue the second cuff-link back to its button. Let the glue dry for a day before you wear the links.

You can make attractive earrings and pins using this technique. Hobby stores and crafts counters in department stores sell earring backs and pin backs to glue onto your favorite buttons. If you are experienced at soldering jewelry, you might try soldering the metal buttons to the link backs, but bear in mind that soldering may discolor some antique buttons.

*Margaret Mohr has an extensive background in pottery making, sewing, weaving, leathercraft, and metalwork. She devotes her time to handicrafts, selling her work to boutiques in and around Boulder and Denver, Colo. Miss Mohr worked for seven years as a costume builder for the New York Shakespeare Festival; her job included making buttons for the Shakespearean costumes.*

Matching gold-and-white antique buttons make a handsome pair of cuff links for a man's dress shirt. The same buttons would make beautiful earrings.

1: Press the shank of the button flat or remove it entirely so the cuff-link backing will fit smoothly to the button.

## Needlecrafts
# Sea-shell buttons

If buttons can be turned into other things, such as jewelry, the reverse is also true: Many found objects can be made into attractive buttons. Sea shells are among the most interesting raw materials to seek. In fact, just searching for shells to use as buttons can add much to your summer or vacation fun. If you are already an inveterate shell collector, button making can at least partially solve the problem of what to do with spare shells.

As veteran collectors know, a good time to hunt for shells at the shore is at low tide, when shells just washed up by the surf are exposed. Some shells are patterned and colored by nature far more beautifully than we could decorate them. If you are lucky enough to find such beauties, you might want to use them as accent buttons on the bodice of a dress, or perhaps as decoration for a belt or handbag. Of course, the types of shells you discover on a beach will depend on the marine life where you live or visit. The readily available pickings for most people tend to be only clam, snail or oyster shells.

For the project pictured, I used baby clam shells, which may also be obtained at fish markets and hobby stores far from the ocean. These small, light-colored shells can be used in their natural color, or dyed to make a more colorful set of buttons. You may want to make matching buttons, using just one type of shell, or you may want to combine different types. Combinations can make striking button sets; just be sure the shells are all about the same size. Try to select shells with natural markings that will give interesting gradations of color, even when they're dyed. When you have collected as many shells as you will need, rinse off all the salt and sand and let them dry thoroughly.

If you plan to dye the shells, as I did, the best dye to use is regular food coloring from your local grocery store. Natural substances tend to take natural dyes better than synthetic dyes. Food coloring also has the advantage of being nonstaining, and it's harmless if swallowed—which makes shell dyeing a safe project for children.

After you have chosen the color you want to use, pour the food coloring into a small bowl. Any bowl you have handy will do except a wooden one, which would absorb the liquid coloring. Before you begin dyeing the shells, it would be a good idea to test the color on a scrap of paper with a small paintbrush. If the color is too dark, you can dilute it by adding a little water, as I did with the blue coloring. The lighter the shade, the more you will see the shell's natural markings. Keep in mind that food coloring, unlike synthetic dyes, dries to only a very slightly lighter tone.

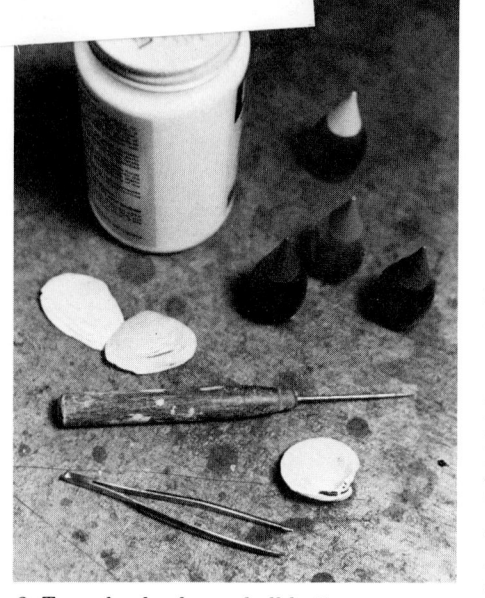

2: To make dyed sea-shell buttons, you will need some small shells (these are baby clam shells), food coloring, a bottle of polymer gel, household tweezers (optional), and a small awl. A small paintbrush may come in handy for final color application.

3: Remember to reposition the tweezers each time you dip; if you don't, you will end up with light spots in the dye where the tweezers gripped the shell.

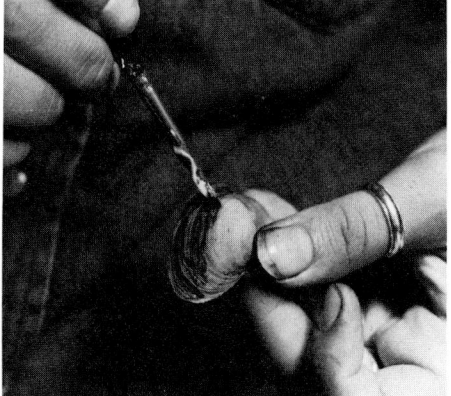

4: Apply a light, even coat of polymer gel. The gel appears opaque when wet, but it dries to a glossy, transparent finish, which will keep colors bright.

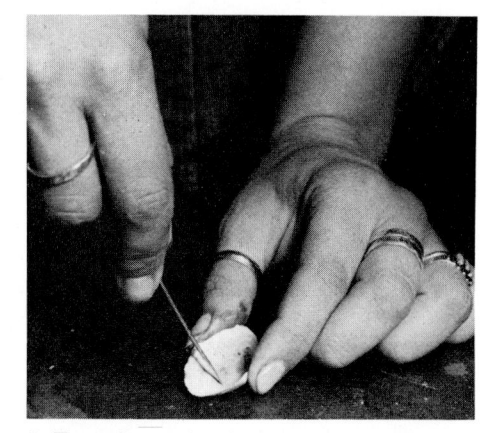

5: To make sewing holes, press and twist with the awl. Be sure to put a piece of scrap wood under the shell so the point of the awl won't damage your tabletop.

Sea shells dyed with food coloring make an original button set. Here, light blue baby clam shells add a charming accent to a handmade Mexican blouse.

When you are satisfied with the color, begin by dipping a shell into the bowl of coloring. For convenience, hold the shell with a pair of household tweezers, as shown in photograph 3, opposite. Continue dipping, occasionally repositioning the tweezers, until you get the shade you want. Let the excess coloring drip into the bowl; then place the shell face up on a paper towel to dry. This won't take long, as food coloring dries in a few minutes. Repeat the dyeing with the rest of the shells.

Many shells become brittle when they dry out and their colors and patterns tend to fade. A coat of polymer gel, from an art-supply store, helps retain the shell's strength and color. Although the gel appears white and opaque in the bottle, it dries to a shiny, transparent finish. Apply it with a small brush (photograph 4), and allow five minutes for drying.

With an awl, an inexpensive tool found at art-supply and hardware stores, make two side-by-side holes in each shell, for sewing (photograph 5). Use scrap wood to back up the shell. Apply even pressure and twist the awl as you work its point through the shell. If the shell is quite hard or thick, you can speed the work by using a small power drill—use the awl to make a small indentation in the shell so the drill won't slip. To keep your fingers free of danger, the shell can be clamped to the piece of scrap wood—use a little masking tape or a few nails, carefully hammered outside the shell's edge. Once the holes are made, you can sew the shells on a shirt or dress to complete the project.

### Needlecrafts
# Buttons made of clay

¢ 🕐 🚶 ✂

Working with clay is particularly satisfying, because you can design clay buttons in many different shapes. Professional potters' clay must be baked in a kiln, but I have used a special clay you can bake in your kitchen oven. Technically, it is a modeling plastic. You can ask for it by that name, or ask for oven-baking clay. If your local art-supply store or hobby shop does not carry it, you can buy it by mail in three-and-a-half-pound blocks. Write to Sculpture House, Inc., 38 East 30th Street, New York, N.Y. 10016. For these projects you will also need a small paintbrush, undercoat, a glaze reducer and the special ceramic glaze finishes used for oven-baking clay. Glazes are sold individually, and can be bought where you purchase the clay. You might start with the three primary colors—red, yellow, and blue—and mix your own secondary colors.

Here are directions for two types of clay buttons—one in a flower shape, the other molded and carved. To begin the flower buttons, break off small chunks of clay and roll them into tiny balls (photograph 6). Flatten all but one ball with your finger to make the petals. One by one, place the flat clay petals around the ball, overlapping them slightly (figure A1, opposite). Then use the awl tip to bend the petals into a pleasing arrangement, which

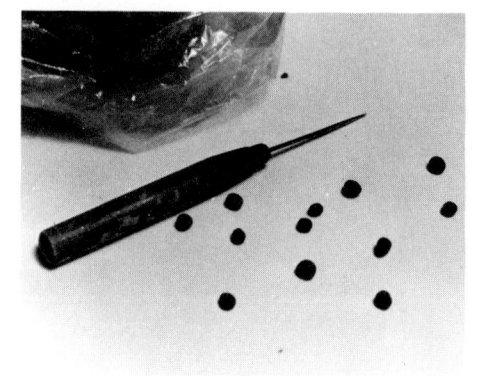

6: Break bits of clay from the block, roll them into balls, and flatten them to make petals of flower. Awl is the only tool you'll need for these buttons.

These delicate-looking clay flower buttons were shaped by hand and painted with pastel yellow, blue, and lilac glazes and salmon-color glaze oxide.

you can vary with each flower. Pierce the base of the flower with the awl, to make the sewing hole (figure A2). When you have made as many flowers as you wish, let them dry for four days. For buttons thicker than those shown, allow a week. If the clay is not thoroughly dry, it will crack when you bake it.

To bake the flowers, put them in a cold oven, and set the temperature at 150 degrees for the first hour. Then turn temperature up to 250 degrees and let the clay bake for another hour. This time, leave the oven door open a crack, for ventilation, so the clay will not bubble.

Once the clay is baked and has cooled, apply the undercoat with a paintbrush, to seal the surface of the porous clay. Let this coat dry for half an hour. Then brush on the glaze (figure A3). To lighten the color, dilute with glaze reducer. I used a yellow glaze, a diluted blue glaze, a diluted mixture of red and blue glazes which gave me lilac, and a dull-finish salmon-color glaze oxide (available only in earth colors).

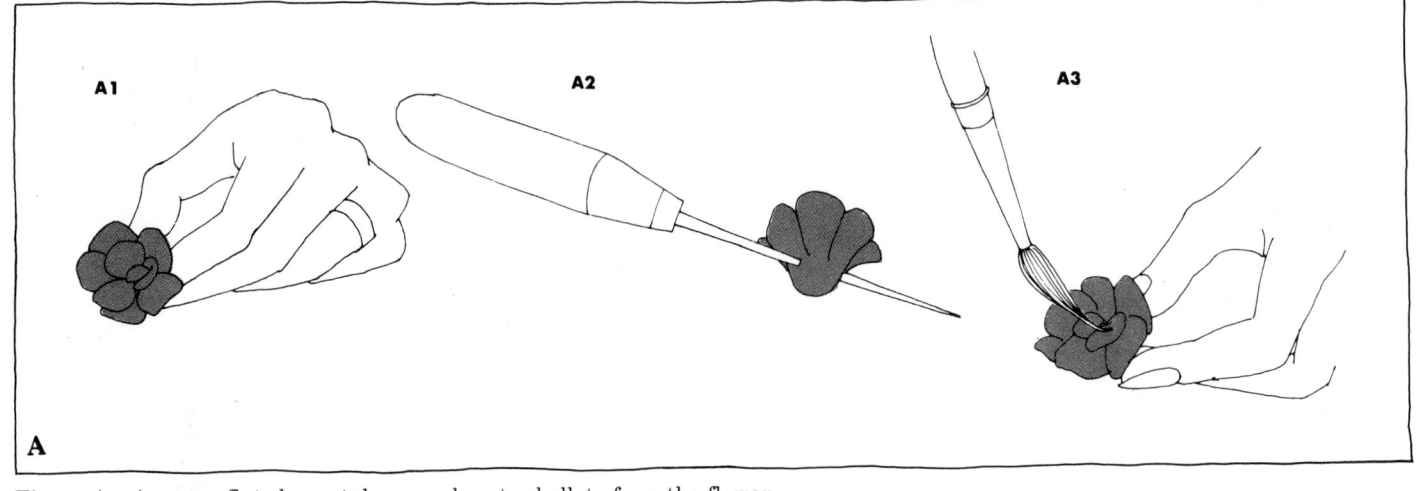

Figure A1: Arrange flat clay petals around center ball, to form the flower.
A2: Use the awl to pierce a sewing hole in base of flower. A3: After baking, apply the undercoat and glaze with the fine-tipped paintbrush.

It's just as easy to mold clay as it is to model it freehand. For the second set of buttons, I used a bottle cap as a mold. To get the shape, press the mold on a chunk of clay and remove excess clay with an awl (photograph 7). Lift off mold; then wet your finger, and smooth the sides of the clay. For carving, I recommend using the awl (photograph 8). I carved an A on one button, a fern leaf on another, and added abstract clay forms to a third. In making your design, remember to allow for the sewing holes. Or, if you have some button shanks, insert them in the clay before it dries. Once your design is completed, follow the baking and glazing procedures for the flower buttons described above.

The author made this rustic trio of clay buttons using a bottle top for a mold. Before baking the clay, she carved designs on two of the buttons, and added clay shapes to the third.

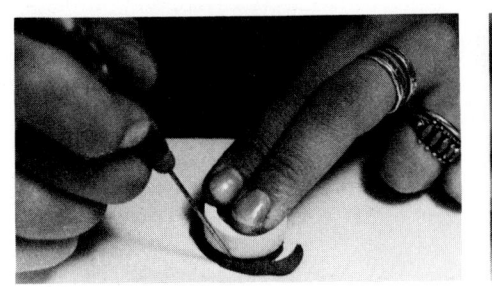

7: Press the bottle-top mold firmly on the clay, and trim away the excess clay with the point of the awl.

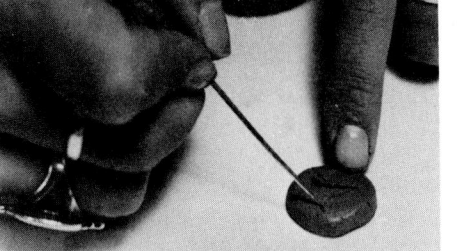

8: It's easy to carve interesting patterns in soft clay, using tip of the ever-handy awl. Baking is the next step.

## Needlecrafts
# Hand-painted buttons

The easiest way to make a figured cloth button is to snap a print fabric into a two-piece button finding. (A button finding is a plastic or metal form, which you cover with fabric to make a button.) The artistic way, however, is to do it all by hand—not only covering the button, but also painting a design on the fabric. The procedure is more complicated, of course, but the results are more original and elegant. And you'll find it's not nearly as hard as you might think.

In a two-stop shopping trip, you can purchase the few materials you'll need that you might not have around the house. At a fabric store, you can buy dressmaker's tracing paper (if you intend to trace a picture on the cloth), a piece of tailor's chalk, and the button findings. The type you

These handmade buttons, with free-form pinwheel asters painted on Chinese silk, are perfect for the lace bodice of a demure Victorian dress.

**B**

Figure B: Sketch shows four steps in making a fastening loop for your fabric buttons. Top three sketches show how to make a basic loop; fourth shows reinforcing of loop with buttonhole stitches, which are a series of loops through which the needle is drawn before being pulled tight.

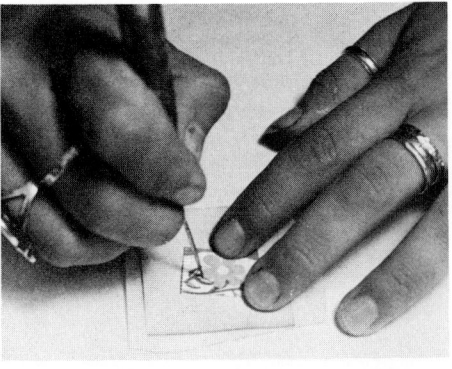

9: Using a piece of dressmaker's tracing paper, outline the picture on the doubled fabric. Make small dots with a needle or the sharp point of an awl.

10: It is a good idea to raise the tracing paper occasionally, without shifting its position, to make sure the pattern is being transferred properly.

11: Center the button finding over the outline, and draw a circle around it with tailor's chalk. Chalk dusts off after you fit the circle over the button face.

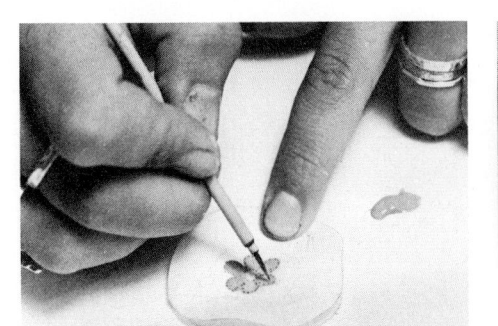

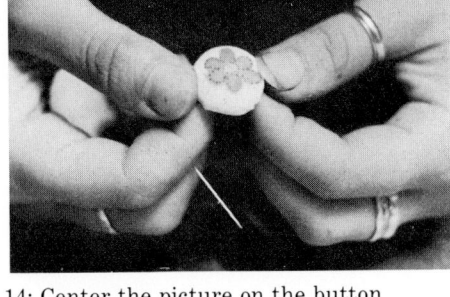

12: Cut the fabric into a circle large enough to fit entirely around the button, and fill in the picture outlines with a fine brush and special fabric paint.

13: After the paint is thoroughly dry, sew the two circular pieces of fabric together, with small gathering stitches, around the perimeter.

14: Center the picture on the button face, using the chalk circle as a guide. Pull the fabric tight at the center of the button back, and stitch.

need comes in one piece and doesn't have a shank. Do not buy the two-piece findings, with shanks, that snap together. At an art-supply store, buy a fine-pointed watercoloring brush and special fabric paint, which is sold in individual colors. This is a water-based paint; but once dry, it will not smudge or wash out.

Making painted buttons is a good way to put solid-color cloth remnants to use. I used an eggshell-color Chinese silk. Photographs 9 through 14 show how these buttons are made. You can draw a design freehand or trace one from a picture. If you use an illustration, be sure it will fit nicely into the circumference of the button finding. Double the fabric, with the right side out. This double thickness is necessary to give the fabric bulk. For working convenience, cut the folded fabric down to a large square.

To transfer a picture to the cloth, place dressmaker's tracing paper face down on the fabric, and lay the picture on the paper. Outline the picture elements by making tiny dots with the point of a needle or an awl. (A tracing wheel is usually too large for this detailed work.) When you remove picture and tracing paper, the picture should be clearly stenciled on the fabric. Center the button finding over it, and draw around the finding with tailor's chalk. Cut the double fabric into a circle, leaving an ample margin around the chalk circle so you can gather the material at the back of the button. Then paint in the outlined design.

When paint is dry, sew the fabric circles together around the perimeter, using gathering stitches. Don't fasten the thread. Center the picture on the face of the button finding; gather fabric tightly in center back; stitch together. To form a loop for sewing on the button, refer to figure B.

For related projects and crafts, see "Ceramics," "Embroidery," "Jewelry," "Sewing," and "Shells."

Beware that you do not lose the substance by grasping at the shadow.

Aesop

# CALLIGRAPHY

## With a Fine Hand

Calligraphy is the art of beautiful handwriting. Distinguished from lettering and penmanship as we know them today, calligraphy is not concerned with any particular set of requirements or rules. It relies chiefly on the personal expression and imagination of the writer. Calligraphers are more interested in the subtle visual impact of writing than in the actual words involved. This goes back to the early history of all writing. As a sacred and mysterious form of expression, writing was an attempt to make visual the spoken word and to capture not only its meaning but also its sound and spirit.

*Herbert Jonas is one of America's most able calligraphers. It is only one of his many artistic accomplishments. He is also an art director, creative director, and book designer; as a costume designer, he has won a number of awards. And he still finds time for travel, for painting, and for sand sculpture at the beach.*

The first development in the history of writing was pictography, which consisted of literal pictures portraying an event. Early cave drawings are an example. Later came ideographs, which represented not only objects but abstract concepts pictorially. The Sumerians, Chinese, Aztecs, Mayans, and Egyptians developed ideographic writing systems. The Egyptians went on to devise a system of phonetic writing that used abstract symbols instead of pictures to indicate speech sounds rather than objects and ideas. This system served as the basis for all Western alphabets. In the East, ideographic writing systems prevailed. But in the West, through refinement and stylization of the ideographs, the once easily recognizable picture forms developed into abstract design elements.

The primary application of fine calligraphy was for the transcription of sacred texts. To the holy men of Arabia, Persia, Israel, China, Japan, and India, as well as to the Christian monks of western Europe, the meaning of the text was held to be in great part dependent on the script in which it was written. A master scribe was well versed in the art of adding overtones to enhance rather than to decorate the holy texts.

Colored pigments and gold leaf were later added to the scribe's palette, enabling him to illuminate—to further elucidate and glorify—the writing. It is interesting to note that illumination is still defined as spiritual enlightenment, as well as a concept of visual light or of lucidity.

Today, calligraphy is not restricted to the appreciation and repetition of the classic styles. New alphabets are designed by the more ambitious calligraphers, and current styles are modified. Modern calligraphy, in most cases, still serves the purpose of being much more than mere writing. It would scarcely be impressive to receive one's academic diploma in the form of a typewritten sheet. Somehow, the fact that a diploma is hand lettered, with decorative flourishes and motifs, makes it more important and of lasting value. Similarly, contrast a motto or proverb printed in a book with the proverb on the opposite page, which has been illuminated. The latter is more meaningful. Pen, brush, ink, paint, and parchment have transformed the motto into a beautiful image; consequently, its meaning is more vivid.

There are endless uses for fine calligraphy, including the making of greeting cards, announcements, invitations, keepsake mottoes, and place cards, and the transcribing of your own writings for private pleasure and for gift giving. Patience and practice will help you master the skills. With creativity and imagination, there is no limit to what you can do.

This hand illumination, by Herbert Jonas, is in a traditional style. The lettering is from the Old English Text alphabet. Instructions for making it begin on page 319.

A sixteenth-century French woodcut shows a monk transcribing a manuscript.

Figure A: The six basic nib shapes. Nibs come in a variety of sizes to produce large or small letters. Many are fitted on the underside with reservoirs that hold a quantity of ink. This cuts down on the time spent reinking.

Figure B: The Old English Text alphabet. Top row, capital letters are all the same height, with the exception of Y, which has a descender (extending below body of letters). Bottom row, lower-case g, j, p, q, and y always have descenders, and b, d, f, h, k, l, and t always have ascenders (rising above body of letters). Practice making letters with square-nib pen held at a 45-degree angle.

## Tools and Materials for Calligraphy

Lettering pens and nibs are available at most art-supply stores. The pen itself should be of good quality, preferably of wood, and have a comfortable grip. Choose the size and style of nib that will produce with the fewest strokes the size alphabet you wish to use. As nibs are not very expensive, it would be a good idea to purchase several types, such as those shown in figure A, and to familiarize yourself with them. Two or three fine sable brushes are essential for painting in letters and illumination, as well as for brush lettering. They come in assorted sizes: No. 1 and No. 2 are most useful. Choose a high-quality waterproof black ink for lettering. For illumination, use either tempera paint or designer's gouache. Before these are used, they are mixed with water to the consistency of heavy cream.

Many types of paper are suitable for calligraphy. Genuine sheepskin, or parchment, is still manufactured, but is expensive. Unless you are an expert, you should not attempt to use it, because mistakes cannot be corrected. Parchment-type papers in various colors are available and are much more practical, as are other fine papers.

You also will need soft pencils, kneaded eraser, compass, dividers, T square, triangle, steel straightedge ruler, tracing paper, and a mechanical fine-line pen for elaborate patterns or adding straight lines.

## The Basic Strokes

To begin, place a square nib in the penholder. You will notice that the nib is divided in the center. The ink flows from the reservoir through this division and onto the paper. To fill the pen nib, fill a small brush with ink, and draw it across the reservoir. This ink will transfer into the nib.

Make a few strokes on scrap paper to use any excess ink. Sit in a relaxed position. Holding the pen nib at an angle of 45 degrees, as illustrated in figure C, practice the vertical stroke. Note that the direction of the stroke is always from top to bottom and that, at all times, the entire surface of the nib's writing edge is in contact with the paper at a 45-degree angle. Now try the strokes shown in figure D. Notice that as you begin and end the curved strokes, the line the nib makes becomes very thin. This is due to the angle at which you are holding the pen and is an essential element of calligraphic alphabets, which make use of thick and thin stroke variation. See the Old English Text alphabet (figure B) and Chancery Cursive (figures G1 and G2, on page 317) for examples of this variation. When you feel confident about making these straight and curved strokes, try to reproduce the more complicated strokes shown in figure E.

These are the basic elements you will need to write the Old English Text alphabet. Repeat all these strokes until you feel comfortable with them. Now practice the alphabet itself. Do not be too concerned if the letters you are making are not precisely the same as those in figure B. Calligraphy, like handwriting, is individual. Your style is your own.

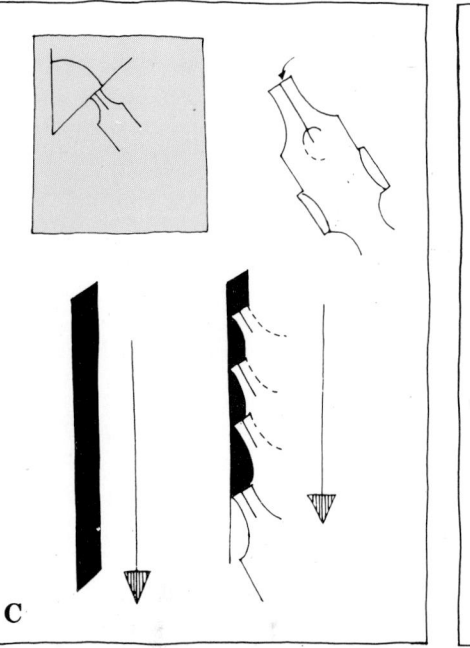

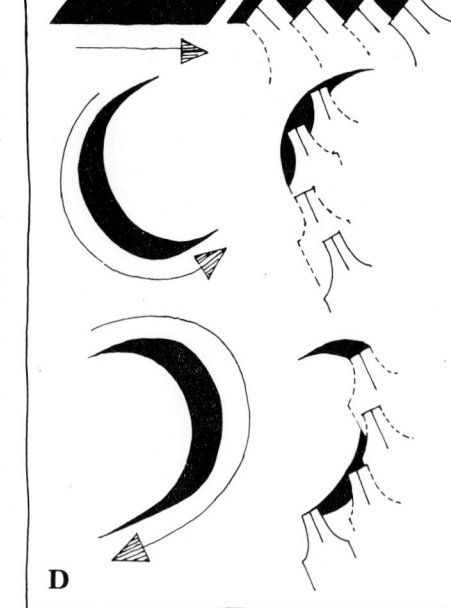

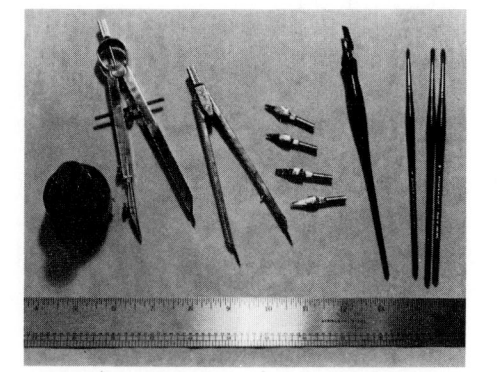

1: The basic supplies of a calligrapher include, left to right: waterproof ink, compass, dividers, an assortment of pen nibs, pen fitted with a nib, a variety of fine sable brushes. At bottom, steel ruler. If you just do ink lettering, brushes are not needed.

Figure C: Draw a 45-degree angle on your work sheet, and position nib along this angle. To make a vertical stroke, move pen downward. Keep pen at constant angle.

Figure D: To make horizontal stroke, top, move pen horizontally, still at a 45-degree angle. Curved strokes are made with the pen nib at the same angle.

Figure E: Elements of Old English Text letters. Once you have mastered these, you can do the alphabet. They look difficult, but you will get them right with practice.

Spacing the letters properly within words and sentences takes a lot of practice. Incorrect spacing will cause illegibility. The best guide to good spacing is your eye. Choose a five-letter word, and write each letter on a separate piece of tracing paper. Move these around until you are pleased with the spacing. To determine space between words, pencil in an o. As with making strokes, practice will enable you to space by eye automatically.

# Chancery cursive

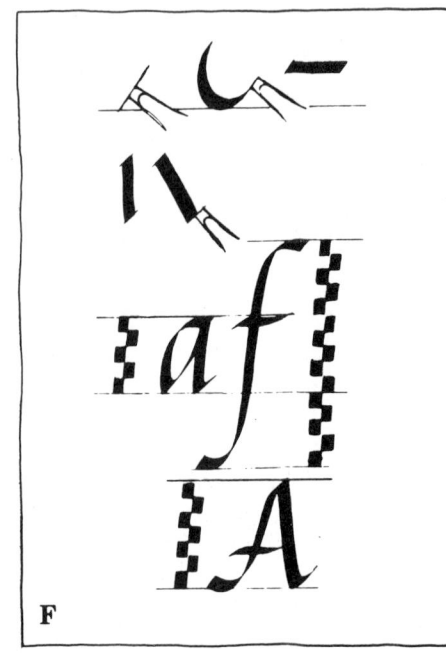

Figure F: Fundamentals of the Chancery Cursive letters. Always position the nib at an angle of 45 degrees. The height of lower-case letters in Chancery Cursive is five widths of the nib you are using. (Nib widths are the zipperlike marks.) Ascenders and descenders are also five nib widths high. Capital letters are seven nib widths each.

The Chancery Cursive alphabet is based on the Humanistic Hand of the fifteenth century. Derived from more informal writing of the period, it exhibits fluidity with a minimum of adornment and seems contemporary in its freshness. It is ideal for the composition of greeting cards, calling cards, and invitations because it gives them an understated elegance. The project described here is an invitation. Substitute your own wording and, if you wish, use paper of a different size or color. The instructions will get you started on the analysis of copy and composition and will familiarize you with this alphabet. What you then decide to compose is up to you.

First, study the alphabet on the opposite page. Note the directionals for each letter and follow the sequence of strokes. Now try to reproduce the letters loosely, without paying too much attention to proportions. When you feel more confident about what your hand and the pen can produce, check figure F and begin to work in correct proportions.

## Copy Analysis
Generally speaking, an invitation expresses several facts in phrase rather than sentence form. Usually, it announces that there will be a party, where it will be held, when it will be held, and so forth. For ready comprehension, it is best to write each fact on a separate, centered line.

Choose a paper size that will work well with the size of letters you plan to use and with the amount of information you need to convey. Your sense of good taste can determine this through experimentation.

With a soft pencil, draw a line down the center of the paper. For each line of copy, draw four horizontal lines five nib heights apart. The need for three spaces to accommodate ascenders and descenders of the Chancery Cursive style is demonstrated by figure F. You could also draw a line

Personally designed invitation, in Chancery Cursive. This alphabet, with graceful ascenders and descenders, was derived from a fifteenth-century calligraphic style.

Figures G1 and G2: The Chancery Cursive alphabet, shown in lower case and in capitals. Numbers and arrows indicate sequence and direction of strokes in each letter. Note variations, such as for e and F.

G

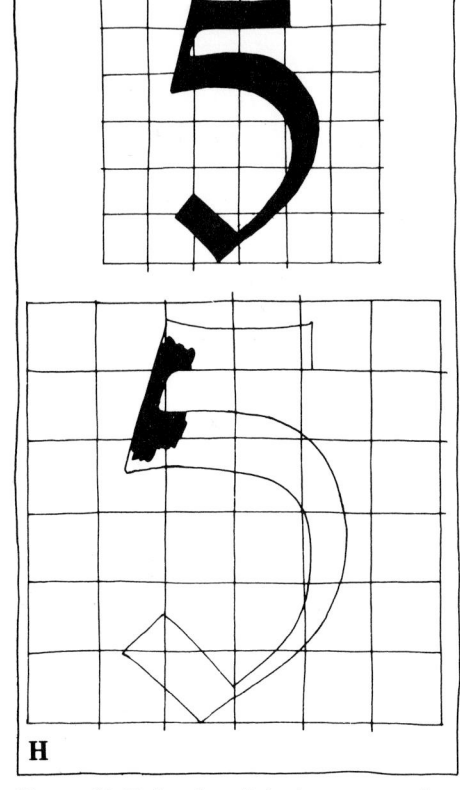

Figure H: Enlarging. Ink character to be enlarged. Then rule a grid of same size squares over it. Rule a larger grid. On it, copy the character square by square.

Figure I: Distorting. Draw characters within a grid. Now draw a distorted grid with the same number of squares; then draw in the distorted characters.

three nib heights below each top line, as a guide for capitals. Space between the lines of copy is dictated by your judgment of final appearance. Ruler, triangle, and T square will help you rule the paper accurately.

Working lightly with the soft pencil, roughly sketch in your copy. Be sure to leave adequate margins at the sides, top, and bottom of the paper to aid in legibility. Work slowly and carefully until you think you have achieved the proper spacing of letters and words. Photograph 2 illustrates roughing in the copy. Do not use a hard lead pencil; it might score the paper and would be difficult to erase. If you work lightly with a soft pencil, you should have no trouble removing the pencil lines when you have finished.

### Inking In Final Copy

Work slowly at all times. Keep a scratch sheet close by. Each time you reink the pen, make a few strokes on the scratch sheet before returning to the project. This will prevent blobbing, which might occur if the pen were overloaded with ink. Any blobs will be on the scratch paper, not the work. Keep the sample of the alphabet (figures G1 and G2, page 317) in front of you, and refer to it frequently as you work. Don't be too concerned if your inked letters are not mechanically identical with those in the sample. You will automatically have a style of your own, and this should be used to its best advantage. If, however, your letters are not at all like those in the sample, you probably need more practice.

As you work, rest your forearm and elbow on the writing table. The pen's movement should result from the movement of your wrist and fingers (see photograph 3). Oriental calligraphers work with their entire arm and shoulder, but in Western calligraphy the wrist controls.

2: A rough pencil sketch of the format is made by ruling a centered vertical line and lines for the copy. Copy is then sketched in to indicate word position.

3: When the rough sketch is refined and word arrangement is visually pleasing, carefully ink in the penciled letters, following figures G1 and G2, page 317.

### Finishing

Once you have inked in all copy, erase the preliminary pencil lines. Using a clean, kneaded eraser, gently remove all pencil marks from the paper. Do not be afraid to erase pencil lines that touch inked letters. The eraser will not affect the ink. If, when marks have been erased, you find a couple of specks that have resisted erasure, try placing a spoonful of dry bread crumbs over them. Gently, with your fingers, rotate the crumbs over the spots. Brush off the crumbs, and the spots should be gone.

Now find or make an envelope suitable for your invitation. Perhaps you would like to letter the address in Chancery Cursive. Remember that if the envelope is smaller than your invitation, you will have to fold your work. The best way is to roll it up and place it in a mailing tube. Once you have mailed it, you have only to wait for the compliments. Your guests will appreciate the time and care that have gone into your creation. You may never again need to buy printed invitations.

## Graphic Arts
# Hand illumination

Hand illumination combines beautiful calligraphy with personal expression and artistry. The technique must express and amplify the copy in an individual and meaningful way. Therefore the illuminator is faced with many options. To begin with, copy must be chosen. In earlier times, there was little opportunity for personal choice in selection of copy, illumination being reserved for the transcription and glorification of holy texts. Today, copy selection is up to the illuminator, who has an endless variety of material to work with, including favorite mottoes, proverbs, quotations, and excerpts from literature, as well as his own writings. It is wise for the beginner to select fairly brief copy so specific techniques of illumination may be utilized, without the complication of having to lay out a great many words or lines of copy. In addition, plan to work with lettering at least three-quarters of an inch high. Letters this size are easier to make than

Illuminated manuscript page entitled "The Visitation," from the Wingfield Horse manuscript, produced in England about 1450. Note the attention paid to color and detail in heightening the beauty of the letters, as well as the artful use of gilding to further enhance the effect. (Courtesy of the Spencer Collection, the New York Public Library, Astor, Lenox, and Tilden Foundations.)

319

smaller ones, as you have a larger area to work with, and this size is effective from the standpoint of display.

Then choose a calligraphic style you believe best expresses the mood of your copy. Within the style, practice the particular letters that you will need to use. Next, select the paints. Tempera paint and designer's gouache are quite good. Both are available in a great many colors, and tempera comes in the silver and gold commonly used by illuminators. Purchase a variety of colors and experiment with them until you have determined which you would like to use for your illumination. Finally, select the paper for your project bearing in mind the suggestions on page 314.

### Making a Traditional Illumination

As illuminations are personal works of art, there are no rules governing technique or procedure. For the benefit of the beginner, I will describe how I created the illumination pictured on page 312. This does not mean that you must follow, line by line, what I have done. After all, illumination started as a very personal form of making the copying of text more beautiful. But if you think it would be helpful for you to copy this example precisely, do so. It will familiarize you with a traditional style of illumination.

The text chosen is a brief proverb of an inspirational nature. The lettering style is Old English Text, which is shown in its entirety in figure B, on pages 314 and 315. The paper is parchment paper in a natural, creamy color. The initial letter B, has been made out of proportion to the rest of the letters and has been illuminated. Elaboration of the initial letter has been the most widely used device in hand-illumination techniques from early days to the present.

As in the preceding project, use a soft pencil to rule off the lines for the copy, including spaces for the ascenders and descenders. Referring to the detail shown on the opposite page, roughly sketch in the enlarged variation of the letter B (see figure H, page 318, for how to enlarge a character). The top of the B should align with the ascenders of the first line; the bottom with the bottom of the letters on the second line, as shown. Follow the directions for photographs 4 and 5, and slowly ink in the letters. When you begin the second line, be sure to indent the first word, to leave space between it and the bottom portion of the B. This is shown in the detail opposite. The third, fourth, and fifth lines should line up at the left with the first line, as shown.

### Detailing the Initial Letter

Following the directions for photograph 6, draw a circle around the initial letter B. The compass shown is equipped with an ink reservoir, so ink is applied as the circle is outlined. If you do not have this type of compass, use one with a soft, sharp pencil to make the circle. Then ink in the line with a mechanical fine-line pen. Referring to the detail opposite, make additional circles and diagonal lines, as needed. Now copy the ribbon motif, making sure the center line, the line around which the vine is twisted, is directly under the center of the circles. On a sheet of scrap paper, practice the shape of the vine pattern. Then work in the vines. Do not be concerned if they are not exactly the same as or in the precise position of those pictured in the detail.

### Painting

With a No. 1 or No. 2 sable brush and water, mix the tempera or designer's gouache to the consistency of heavy cream. Use the No. 1 brush to prepare a large area, such as the tail of the ribbon, for paint. Coat the fine brush with paint, and draw a line of color just inside the black outline, all around. Now you can use the larger brush to fill in the area without fear of going past the black outline. Apply all paint quite firmly, in continuous strokes, so that each painted area appears to be a flat, solid area of color. Fill in all areas, as in the detail, using the colors shown or

4: Ink slowly and very carefully, with the pen at a 45-degree angle. Place a sheet of scrap paper under your hands to protect the parchment.

5: Dividers indicate the space occupied by lower-case letters, exclusive of ascenders and descenders. This is one-third of the total space ruled.

6: Draw a square around the initial letter. Then draw two diagonal lines through the square to determine the midpoint. Place compass point here, as shown, and draw a circle around letter.

improvising with additional or substituted colors. The paints dry rapidly. For a final touch, follow the directions for photograph 7.

Further projects will depend on your artistic interpretation. If you prefer traditional styles, refer to religious documents or historical sources. If not, use your imagination and the techniques described here. Eventually, you may develop techniques of your own.

For related entries, see "Gold Foil and Leafing," "Greeting Cards," and "Silkscreen Prints."

Detail of the initial letter of the hand illumination shown in its entirety on page 312. The vines and flowers soften the geometrics and enhance the copy.

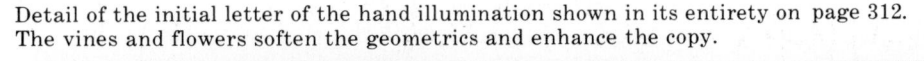

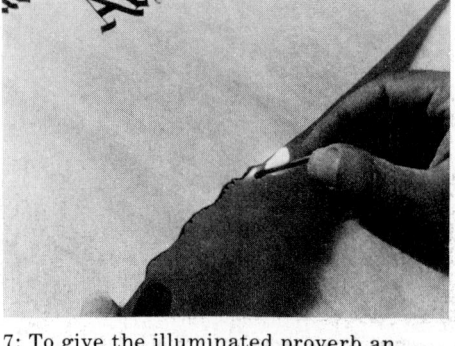

7: To give the illuminated proverb an antique look, singe the border slightly with the flame of a match. Hold the flame at the very edge of the parchment paper. Blow out the flame as soon as the paper catches fire. The edge should be browned and burned off just a bit. Continue around edge until it is evenly singed. Practice on a scrap sample first.

# CAMERAS
# Two You Can Build

The first camera was conceived as a sketching aid sometime in the early 1600s. It consisted quite simply of a dark chamber with a small hole at one end, through which light was projected onto the opposite interior wall. There an inverted image of the outside scene was formed, which an artist, working inside the chamber, traced. The inventor of this dark chamber, or camera obscura, is not known but it is certain that Aristotle was familiar with the principle and Leonardo da Vinci made precise drawings of the camera obscura.

Later models were built on sedan chairs or on wheels for movability. About 1660, a compact model was designed, with a lens instead of a hole and an interior mirror to reflect the image onto a ground-glass screen.

Some 60 years later, in 1727, Johann H. Schulze, a German physicist, discovered that silver salts are sensitive to light. A century passed before Joseph Nicephore Niepce, a French scientist, made use of that discovery to take the first photograph.

Niepce placed a pewter plate treated with silver salts in a camera obscura and exposed the plate for eight hours. The result of his experiment was a crude, barely discernible view of a building outside his window. Yet, unlike the images produced by previous cameras obscura, it was permanent.

A partner of Niepce, Louis J. M. Daguerre, went on to develop a more efficient process of photography. Daguerre used a light-sensitive metal plate, which he developed with mercury vapor. His process, which he announced in 1839, became known as daguerreotype and was an important milestone in the development of modern photography.

The camera obscura today is more than a clever sketching device. A periscope, for example, is basically a form of the camera obscura, as is the viewing mechanism on a single-lens reflex camera. In its basic form, however, the camera obscura, with a sheet of tracing paper, provides an entertaining way of transforming even the most hesitant sketcher into an artist. And in the form of a pinhole camera, which today uses fast modern films, it furnishes an instructive basic aid for learning the fundamentals of photography.

*Stuart M. Penney is a self-taught professional photographer. In 1958, he began his own custom photographic-finishing service, now a photographic-supply and specialty store located in the Gramercy Park area of New York. Stuart gives private photography lessons and teaches on occasion in the New York public schools. He is a native of New York City.*

## Graphic Arts
## Making a camera obscura

$ ▯ ⚇ ⚒

The dimensions of a camera obscura are determined by the focal length of its lens; so, in listing the materials needed, I can only approximate their measurements. More on the subject of focal length in a moment.

The magnifying glass should be round and no less than 2 inches in diameter. In general, the bigger the glass, the brighter the image. If you already have a large, expensive glass—the ideal kind—you can use it as a detachable lens without damage to it or its frame. More practical, however, and nearly as good would be a smaller, dime-store glass.

The mirror could be the nonmagnifying side of a small, round shaving mirror or something similar, 3 to 6 inches in diameter.

Use heavy cardboard to construct a solid, rigid box. Double- or triple-thickness matte board is excellent.

A good glazier can supply the ground-glass screen. Ask for ground glass or frosted glass—the kind that appears to have been sanded on one side. A fair-size pane should cost less than a dollar. An acceptable substitute is a sheet of clear plastic frosted on one side.

The other materials and tools may be found around the house: masking tape, a ruler, a pencil, a single-edge razor blade or a utility knife.

1: Materials and tools needed for making a camera obscura are: heavy, rigid cardboard, a magnifying glass, a small mirror, a pane of frosted glass or plastic, masking tape, a ruler, a pencil, and a single-edge razor blade.

Pinhole cameras (see page 327) take excellent pictures like these. Since
exposures are long, only landscapes and still subjects are suitable for taking
pictures with the pinhole camera. The camera must be held absolutely steady.

Position the magnifying glass between some bright object, such as a lamp, and a sheet of paper. Slowly move the glass toward the paper. When the glass is close enough, it will produce an inverted image of the object on the sheet. As the distance between glass and paper changes, the clarity of the image varies. When the image is at its sharpest, it is said to be in focus. This distance is the focal length of the lens.

In terms of shape, a camera obscura is a cube, each side of which is equal to the focal length of its lens (the magnifying glass, that is). Thus, before building a camera obscura, you must first determine the focal length of your glass. To do so, produce an inverted image as you did before, this time with a ruler placed as in figure A to measure the exact distance between the glass and the paper.

Focus on an object about 12 to 15 feet distant. The focal length depends not only on the size of the magnifying glass, but also on the distance between the object and the sheet of paper. Because the camera obscura will be nonadjustable, it must be built with a compromise focal length as its basic dimension. An object 12 to 15 feet away will yield a workable average focal length.

You will probably determine the focal length of your magnifying glass to be between 6 and 12 inches. Whatever it is, you will use that measurement to determine the length and width of each side of your camera obscura, which, as I have noted, will be a cube. The focal length of my glass, which was 2½ inches in diameter, was 8 inches.

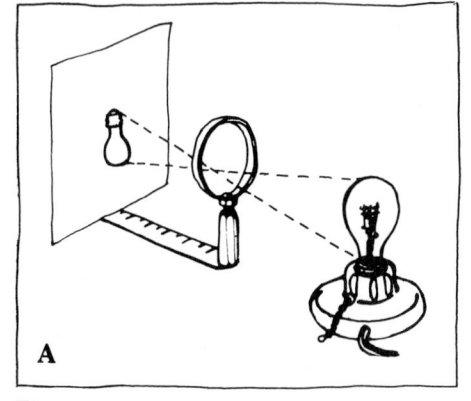

Figure A: This sketch illustrates the way to determine the effective focal length of your lens, the magnifying glass. The distance between lamp and lens should be about 15 feet. Distance between lens and paper dictates the dimensions of your camera obscura.

2: To make it easy to fold the heavy cardboard, cut a groove along each folding line by slicing slightly to each side of the line at a 45-degree angle.

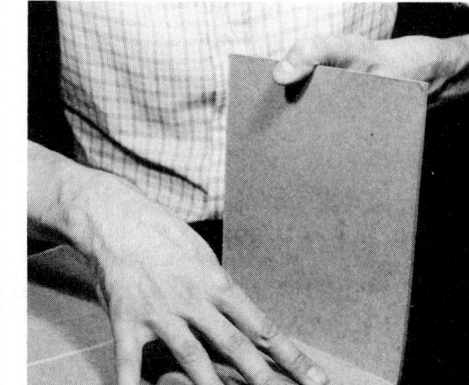

3: Bend the T-shape cardboard upward along the grooved lines, so that each of the three square sides is standing in a vertical position.

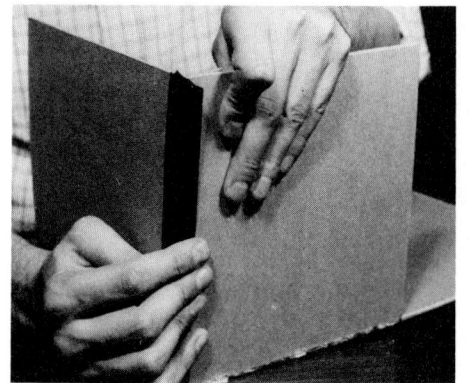

4: Tape meeting edges of the cardboard to hold the upright sides together. Also tape the folded edges at the bottom of the box to reinforce them.

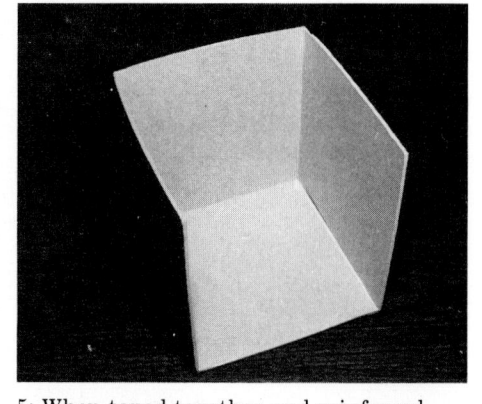

5: When taped together and reinforced, the camera-obscura housing should look like a cube with two of its sides—the top and the front—missing.

The camera obscura has an extremely shallow depth of field. The image is sharpest at the center. Quality of image is governed by quality of lens.

This is the way your camera obscura will look when it is completed. A better image is obtained if the scene to be viewed is bright and the camera obscura is in a shaded or dim spot.

I thus determined the dimensions of my camera obscura: 8 inches by 8 inches by 8 inches. If the focal length of your magnifying glass is different, the dimensions of your camera obscura will be different.

Of the six surfaces of the camera obscura, four (the two sides, the back, and the bottom) will be solid cardboard, with no openings. The fifth surface (the front) will also be cardboard, but will have an opening large enough to accommodate the lens. The sixth and last surface (the top) will be the ground-glass screen.

Let us consider the four solid-cardboard surfaces first. If you prefer working with individual pieces of cardboard, cut four squares, each measuring one focal length by one focal length (8 by 8 inches, in my case). If—as I did—you use one large piece of cardboard, cut out a pattern of four adjacent squares, clustered in the form of a T. Again, each square should be one focal length by one focal length.

To facilitate fitting separate squares together, bevel edges with a single-edge razor blade. If you cut out a T pattern, groove the three edges of the center square that it shares with the three outer squares.

Fold the cardboard so that it assumes the shape of a cube with two sides missing. Using black masking tape, first tape corners where edges meet; then tape the three folded edges for reinforcement (photograph 4). Camera shops sell this tape. At this point, the project should appear as it does in photograph 5. If you use four separate squares of cardboard, they are, of course, taped together the same way.

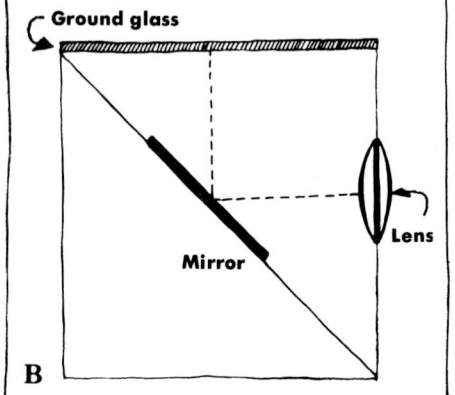

Figure B: This is a cross-section of the camera obscura, showing the diagonal mirror. The distance from lens to mirror, plus the distance from mirror to screen, equals the length of one side of the square—one focal length.

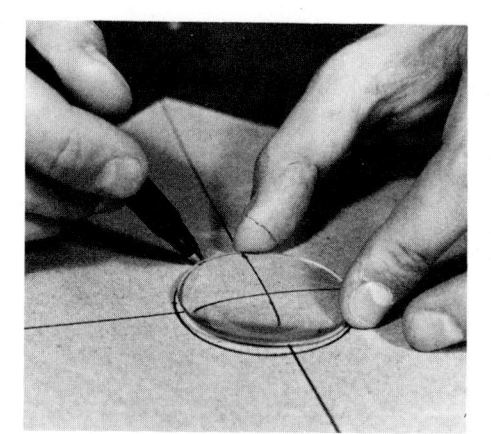

6: After drawing the diagonals of the front, place the lens over the center, and trace its outline. Then cut out a hole in which to fit the lens.

7: Tape the lens in place; then tape the front to the camera-obscura body. Be careful not to cover more of the lens than necessary with the tape.

Cut a fifth square of cardboard, and determine its center by drawing its diagonals. If possible, remove the magnifying glass from its frame; place it over the center of the square, and trace its outline with a pencil (photograph 6). If you can't remove the frame, trace the outline of the frame itself. Cut along the outline, and position the lens in the hole, taping it with small pieces of tape on both sides to keep it in place (photograph 7). Bevel the edges of the square, and tape it to the other three.

8: Cardboard holding the mirror should be wide enough just to fit inside the body and as long as the diagonal of a square side. Center and tape the mirror.

9: Fit cardboard holding the mirror in a diagonal position in the box. The mirror should face toward the lens. Tape the cardboard piece in place.

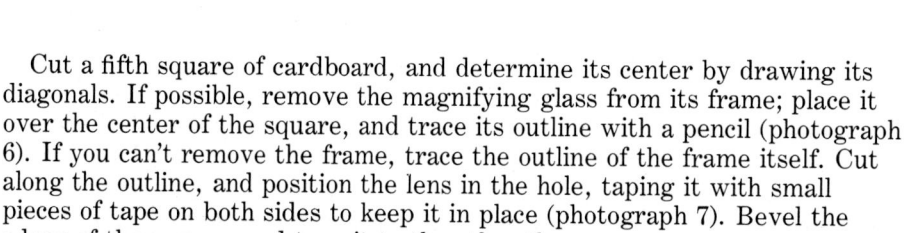

10: Place the ground-glass screen, frosted side down, over the top of the camera obscura. After checking the image, tape all four edges to the cardboard.

Measure the diagonal of a square; then cut a cardboard rectangle that length and slightly less in width (to allow for cardboard's thickness) than one focal length. Tape the mirror in the center of this rectangle (photograph 8). Fit the rectangle into the box, with the mirror facing toward the lens, as shown in photograph 9. Tape in place.

The ground-glass screen, which should be the same size as the other squares, may now be placed on top, frosted side down (photograph 10). Before taping the edges, check the image by pointing the box at a lamp or window. If the image is dim, remove the screen and make sure its surfaces are clean. Painting the cardboard interior of the box flat black will brighten the image. When you obtain a satisfactorily clear image, tape the screen in place, and you are ready to trace the image you see.

## Graphic Arts
# Making a pinhole camera

A pinhole camera is nothing more than a cardboard box with a pinhole "lens," covered with a flap which acts as a shutter in the front and a frame in the back to accommodate sheet film. Yet if you build one with care and precision, it will be a device enjoyable in itself, instructive in the fundamentals of photography, and capable of taking pictures like those on page 323 and the one to the right.

You will need a large piece of rigid cardboard, 14 inches by 26 inches, black on at least one side. Black matte board is ideal. You will also need black masking tape. Both are available at any photographic-supply store. Some regular household white glue is also required. A 1-inch square of aluminum foil will do for your lens.

The tools you will use are household items: a No. 10 sewing needle, a single-edge razor blade, or utility knife, a ruler, a pencil, a sheet of extra-fine sandpaper, and a candle.

Cut a strip of cardboard 7 by 26 inches. With the ruler and pencil, divide the strip into four sections, as follows: 7 by 7 inches, 6 by 7 inches, 7 by 7 inches, and 6 by 7 inches. This strip will form the body of your camera (see figure C).

From the remaining strip of cardboard, cut four rectangles, each 6 by 7 inches. Set one rectangle aside for use later at the camera back. In a second rectangle, cut a hole about ½ inch square. Be careful to place the hole in the exact center of the rectangle; this is the spot where diagonal lines drawn on the rectangle cross.

In the center of one of the other two rectangles, cut a rectangular hole, 4 by 5 inches; in the center of the other, cut a smaller rectangular hole, 3½ by 4½ inches. You now have two cardboard frames: one 1 inch wide, the other, 1¼ inches wide (see figure D).

The pinhole camera has extreme depth of field. Everything is the same degree of focus, from near to far, but focus is soft, giving pictures a moody quality.

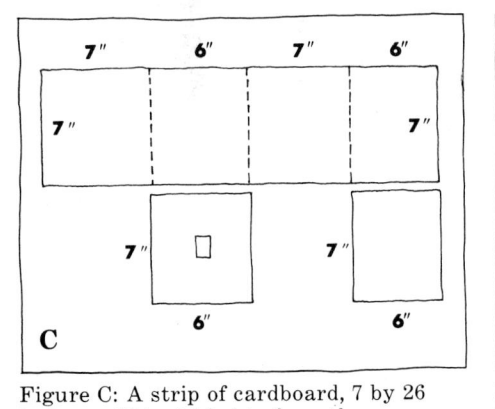

Figure C: A strip of cardboard, 7 by 26 inches, will be folded to form the camera body. Two 6-by-7-inch rectangles, one with a small hole in its center, will become the front and back.

Figure D: Two 6-by-7-inch rectangles form the film holder. In one, cut a hole 4 by 5 inches; in the other, cut a hole 3½ by 4½ inches. Glue the two pieces together, making a frame to hold the film.

Place the wider of the two frames (the one with a 1¼-inch border) on a flat surface. If only one side of the cardboard is black, be sure the black side is face down.

Coat one side (either side will do) of the narrower frame with glue. Then position this frame, glue side down, over the wider frame, so the outside edges of both frames coincide. Press the frames together, and apply pressure for a few minutes until the glue begins to adhere. Wipe off any glue that oozes out and apply pressure until the glue dries.

This double-thickness cardboard will be attached later to the camera back and will serve as a holder for the sheet film.

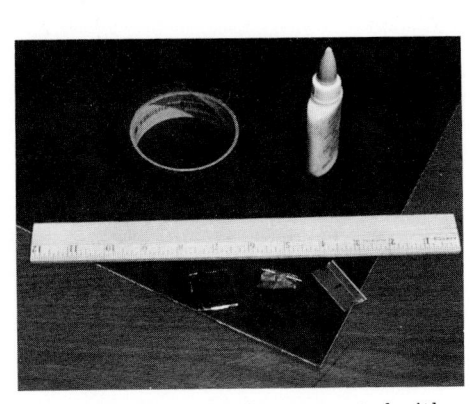

11: A pinhole camera is constructed with rigid cardboard (black on at least one side), black tape, foil, glue, a No. 10 sewing needle, a single-edge razor blade, a ruler, a pencil, some extra-fine sandpaper, and a candle.

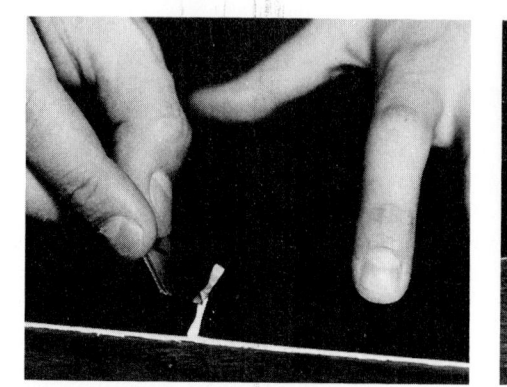

12: Prepare the cardboard strip for folding by cutting, on cardboard's black side, shallow grooves along the three lines dividing the four sections.

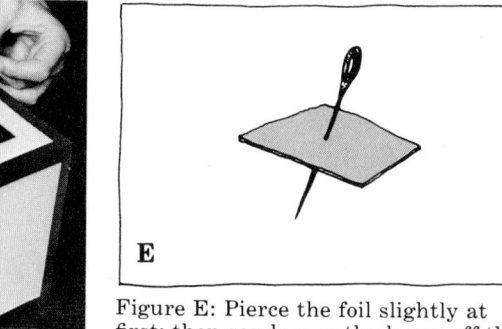

13: Before folding strip to form camera body, bevel both 7-inch ends, on black side of cardboard. This will make a tight corner where these ends meet.

This is the finished pinhole camera. The flap that functions as the shutter is shown folded to admit light for picture taking. If you construct the camera carefully, you will avoid light leaks that would ruin the photographs.

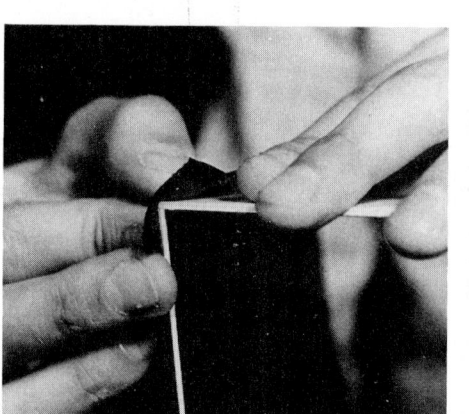

14: Fold the cardboard strip, with the black side inside, to form an open-ended box. Tape the ends together; then tape folded corners to reinforce them.

15: The four-sided camera body should be rigid enough to stand by itself. Inspect all the edges for tiny light leaks, and tape over any leaks you find.

Making the camera body is simply a matter of folding the cardboard strip (the one measuring 7 by 26 inches) into the shape of a box. First, cut V-shape grooves along the three lines dividing the four sections, to make the folding easier, and bevel the two 7-inch ends. Grooves and bevels should be on the black side of the cardboard. Fold the strip, and tape all four corners for reinforcement (see photographs 12, 13, 14).

16: Tape the film holder (figure D, page 327) to one end of the body so the frame that will later hold the film sheet is facing away from the interior.

**E**

Figure E: Pierce the foil slightly at first; then sandpaper the burrs off the dimpled side. Next, work the needle about half its length through the foil to produce an even, round pinhole. Careful, precise work is critical because the pinhole acts as the lens for the camera. If the aperture is too large, the image will not be as sharply focused.

Tape the film holder (the two cardboard frames glued together) to one end of the camera body (photograph 16). The indentation formed by the two glued frames should face outward. Position the camera back (the solid 6-by-7-inch cardboard rectangle) over the film holder, black side facing inward, and tape one of the 6-inch edges to the camera body to form a hinge (photograph 17). A small piece of tape attached to the other 6-inch edge will keep the back closed when the camera is loaded with film.

To the other end of the camera body, tape the camera front (the 6-by-7-inch cardboard rectangle with the ½-inch-square hole in it). Again, the black side should face the interior.

Place the square of aluminum foil on a soft, flat surface—an old newspaper on a tabletop will do. Pierce the center of the foil with a No. 10 sewing needle. Do so carefully and slowly. A piece of tape attached to each side of the foil will help in making a smooth, round hole; later, the tape is discarded. Sandpaper the dimpled side of the pierced foil to remove the tiny burrs. Then work the needle through the hole again, this time about halfway up its shank (see figure E).

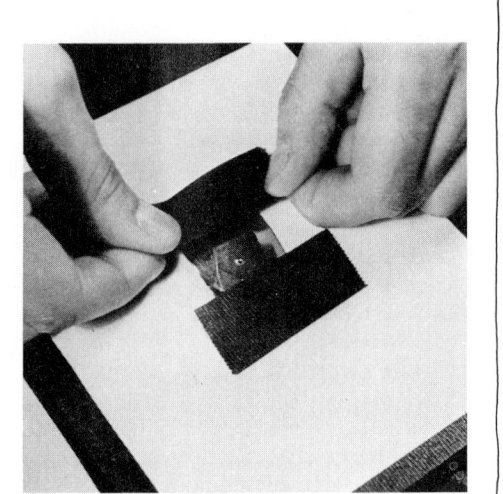

17: Hinge the top of the camera back over the film holder. It is extremely important for this back to fit tightly and smoothly, so there are no light leaks.

18: Tape the camera front to the body. Blacken both sides of the foil; center the pinhole over the hole in the camera front, and tape the foil in place.

Blacken both sides of the foil by passing them over a candle flame. Position the pinhole, the dimpled side facing inside, over the center of the hole in the camera front. Tape the foil in place (photograph 18). Cut a 3-inch square of cardboard; center it over the pinhole, and hinge it along the bottom with a strip of tape. This is the shutter. A small piece of tape at the top will keep it closed when the camera is not in use.

Load the camera with 4-by-5-inch sheet film in an absolutely dark room or closet. When loading the film, be sure the notches in the sheet are at the upper left corner of the camera (figure F); that way, you will know the emulsion side of the film is on the inside, as it should be.

To take a picture, lower the front flap briefly. This exposes the film. In bright sunlight, with fast black-and-white film such as Tri-X Pan, try an exposure time of one to two seconds; in bright, overcast weather, increase time to two to four seconds. With color-negative film, triple the time. If possible, bracket an exposure by taking two more shots, one at half and one at double the initial time. At first, you will guess times; later, when you have developed your first photographs, you will have a standard by which to estimate exposure times accurately.

During exposures, keep the camera steady by taping or weighting it down. Still lifes and landscapes are excellent subjects; they provide the soft, dreamy quality characteristic of the best pinhole photographs.

For a related entry, see "Photography."

**F**

Figure F: The notches in sheet film help position it in the dark: they should be at the upper left corner of the camera. In the field, use a large loading bag, available from a photographic-supply store, when you load film.

# CANDLEMAKING
## Dip, Cast, Decorate

*Anita Wharton, a commercial artist for Lebhar Freidman Incorporated, is also a free-lance photographer and amateur oil painter. She began making candles as a hobby, under the tutelage of a friend. Her hobby grew into a business, and she has sold many candles at art exhibits and craft fairs.*

Candlemaking requires a minimum of skill and is something anyone can do, including children, provided they are well supervised. Materials for making candles are available at hobby shops. The type of wax sold at supermarkets—paraffin for sealing preserve jars—makes acceptable candles, and for convenience I use it in the children's project below, but it costs more and is not as good as standard candle wax. For really good candles, buy slabs of white, ready-to-use commercial wax at a hobby shop. Experience will teach you how much wax is needed for a given candle, but as a general guide, a ten-pound slab of raw wax will make four quart-size candles.

Candlewicks are made of braided cotton yarn that has been treated and coated with a thin layer of wax. They are sold in lengths cut from spools and in two or three widths—medium for the average candle, extra thin and extra thick for candles in special sizes.

Stearic acid, an optional wax additive commonly used in making candles, is sold in granule form at hobby shops. It makes wax more opaque, stronger in color, and slower burning. It is added after the wax has been melted. The correct proportion is 20 percent by weight.

Scent oils, added just before the candles are poured into molds, is another optional additive. The fragrance is especially strong immediately after a scented candle has been snuffed out. Bayberry— especially appropriate for Christmas candles—and other essences formulated specifically for wax, such as pine and sandalwood, are sold at many hobby shops. If unavailable locally, you can order from Berje, 43-10 23rd Street, Long Island City, N.Y. 11101.

Wax is flammable, so it is essential that you take every precaution when you are melting it. Use a double boiler; most wax melts at between 110 and 200 degrees Fahrenheit, and a double boiler will keep its temperature from exceeding the boiling point of water (212 degrees Fahrenheit). Never leave melted wax over an open flame unattended, and don't pour or cast it near an open flame. To extinguish wax fires, always keep powdered baking soda handy. Don't use water to extinguish a wax fire should one occur.

In the children's project that follows, a tin can set in a pot of water is used as a makeshift double boiler. It is safe, as long as you boil the water slowly over a low flame (or at the low setting on an electric range) and turn off the heat as soon as the last bit of wax has melted. Crayons were used for coloring the wax. This is fine for children, but for the more acceptable candle-coloring techniques, see page 336.

### Carving and Molding
## Hand-dipped candles  ¢ ☒ 👪 🕯

A simple project for children demonstrates the age-old method of hand dipping candles. The original process consisted of dipping a weighted wick repeatedly in a vat of molten wax. The basic process remains unchanged, but I would like to show you how to make two hand-dipped candles, using everyday objects and materials, and two large, molded candles as by-products of the dipping. Although this is a project easy enough for children, it is vital they have constant adult supervision for safety sake.

You will need two 32-ounce fruit-juice cans, some cooking oil (or a can

The candlemaking projects include these pastoral, wild-flower-and fern-decorated white candles. Instructions for making them are on page 341.

1: Tin cans and pans act as double boilers for melting wax. Overheated wax can be dangerous, so extinguish heat as soon as last bit of wax has melted.

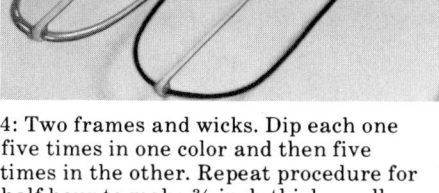

2: Placing chunk of wax in can. If you must add more wax after you have melted some, be careful to place it gently, so molten wax does not spatter.

Hand dipping is probably the simplest way of making candles. These were dipped by a child, with adult supervision, and were made of alternating layers of red and purple wax. This will create interesting dripping patterns as the candles burn.

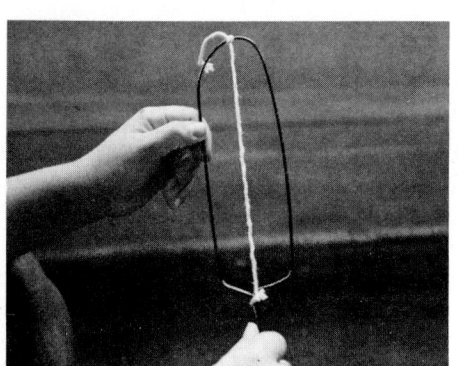

3: Bend wire hangers to this shape, and position the wick, as shown. Be sure it is stretched as taut as possible so wax will not bend as it builds up.

4: Two frames and wicks. Dip each one five times in one color and then five times in the other. Repeat procedure for half hour to make ¾-inch-thick candles.

of spray silicone or petroleum jelly), two large saucepans, three 16-ounce boxes of unrefined paraffin (sold in supermarkets), two wire coat hangers, about 4 feet of medium-size wick, two wax crayons in different but coordinating colors, a pair of scissors, and an ice pick (or piece of wire hanger). Follow these step-by-step instructions:

Clean the insides of the cans, and wipe with a thin coat of cooking oil.

Place the cans in 3 inches of water in the saucepans (photograph 1).

Cut the wax into chunks small enough to fit easily into the cans, and drop in enough wax to fill the cans (photograph 2).

Heat the water to boiling, and turn down the flame so the water will remain at a low boil. While the wax is melting, you can prepare the hangers.

Bend hangers to the shape shown, and tie on wicks (photographs 3 and 4).

When all the wax has melted, check the liquid-wax levels. They should be an inch below the can rims. If not, add more wax and wait for it to melt.

Remove the paper from the crayons, and drop them into the cans— one color in one can and the other in the other can (photograph 5). Wait for the crayons to melt, and then stir the wax gently to diffuse the color.

Turn off the flame, and wait about 15 minutes for the molten wax to cool.

Dip the wire frames and wicks into the wax (up to within an inch of the wick end), pull out, and hang to let the wax solidify. We hung the frames on a laundry rack, photograph 6. As the molten wax in the cans cools further, it will not be necessary to set the frames aside after each dipping. The wax will solidify quickly enough for you to simply hold the frame over the can for a few seconds, and then dip again (photograph 7). About half an hour of repeated dipping will complete the candles.

When the wax deposit has grown thick enough (about ¾ inches), hang the frames for the final drying period—about an hour, or until wax is firm.

With scissors or a knife, cut through the wicks at the top and the wax and wicks at the bottom, to free the candles from the frames.

You can turn the remaining liquid wax into candles by putting the cans in the refrigerator. When the wax has solidified, remove it from the cans by dipping them in hot water. To add wicks, push a heated ice pick or straight piece of wire hanger all the way down into the candles; insert the wicks (see photograph 14, page 336), and seal the openings with some melted wax.

Ten-year-old David Hunter begins dipping. He submerges frame up to an inch below wick end and withdraws it, all in one movement. Be sure stove is turned off.

5: Adding crayons—red to one can and purple to the other. You can make solid-color candles with one can, one crayon.

6: Wax-coated frames cooling on rack. Middle column is candle. Wax on frames can be scraped off with knife and reused.

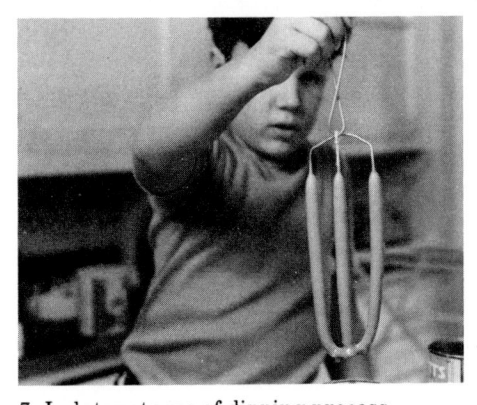

7: In later stages of dipping process, hold frame over can for a few seconds until wax solidifies; then redip.

No need to be wary of
these beehives. They
are rolled wax, painted and cut to look
like whimsical versions of hives.

## Carving and Molding
# Beeswax honeycomb candles ¢ ☒ ☉ ♨

Since ancient times, people have regarded bees as models of industry and purity. For that reason, and because it is so sweet smelling, beeswax has always been used for church and temple candles. To this day, church candles usually contain at least 50 percent beeswax. You can buy beeswax in blocks for making candles in molds, but this project shows you how to make very simple candles by rolling thin sheets of honeycombed wax.

In its natural honeycomb form, beeswax would be ideal for a rolled candle, but you probably would have to go straight to the source (a beehive) to find enough of it. In its place, I use commercially produced part-natural beeswax that has been embossed with a honeycomb pattern. It comes in 8-by-16-inch sheets in a variety of colors and is available at many hobby shops. If you have difficulty obtaining it, you can order it from A. I. Root, 1106 East Grand Street, Elizabeth, N.J. 07201.

To make a 5-inch candle 2 inches in diameter, you will need one 8-by-16-inch sheet of wax, a pair of scissors, and 7 inches of wicking.

Fold and tear the sheet of wax in half lengthwise (photograph 9). Place a piece of 7-inch wick at one short end. Fold half an inch of the edge over the wick. Crimp the wax so it holds the wick snugly. Roll the wax at a slight angle to make a conical shape at the wick end. Before the end of the sheet is reached, overlap it with the end of the other cut sheet. Finish rolling.

Beehives are the source of very fine wax for making candles. Natural beeswax burns evenly and is sweetly fragrant.

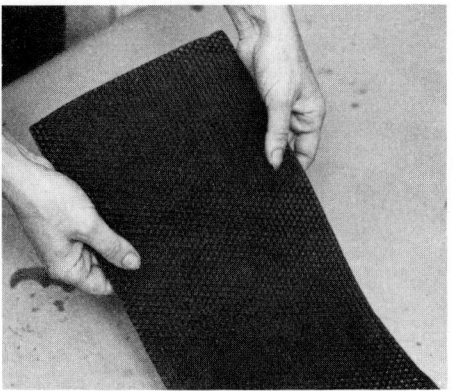

8: A sheet of 8-by-16-inch honeycomb wax. You can make a 9-inch candle by rolling it lengthwise or a 17-inch candle by rolling it across its width.

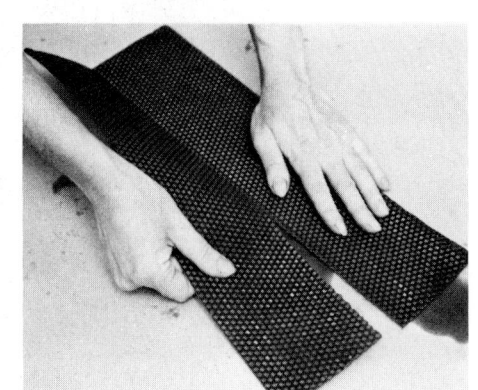

9: Fold the sheet of wax lengthwise, and tear along the fold. Both 4-by-16-inch pieces are needed to make a 2-inch-thick and 5-inch-high honeycomb candle.

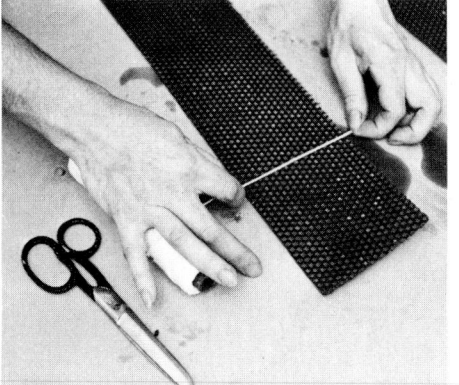

10: Use a piece of wick about 3 inches longer than the width of the wax sheet. You can cut off the excess wick at both ends after the candle is rolled.

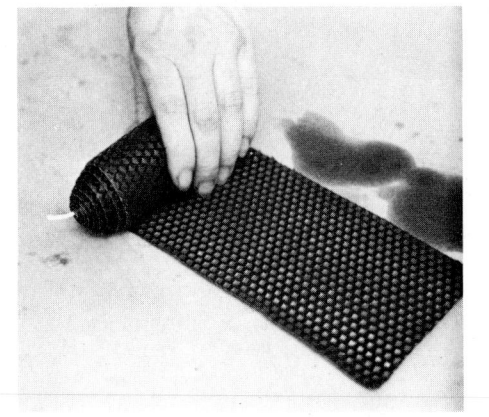

11: Roll the wax fairly tightly at a slight angle to create pointed end. The wax will bend easily and hold its cylindrical shape without any sealing.

## Carving and Molding
# Confectionary candles

One of the nicest characteristics of wax is that it can be a great impersonator. It especially lends itself to the imitation of such delicious edibles as ice-cream sundaes, sodas, and whipped cream. These confectionary delights made of wax may not be taste treats, but they are colorful and make lively decorative additions to a room. You can learn to concoct your own confectionary candles by following these instructions.

Although, in the children's project, I showed you how to color wax with crayons, they are not recommended for general use, because they often contain chemicals that impair the even burning of the wax. Ordinary food color and commercial dyes are also undesirable, since they color unevenly and often leave residue. It is best to color wax with products designed for that purpose. Candle color in both liquid and cake form is sold at hobby shops. Follow the directions included to use either correctly.

To make the ice-cream-sundae candle in the color photograph, far right, you will need enough wax in each color to half fill a medium-size sauce pan (see

Miss Wharton enjoys making extravagant "ice-cream" concoctions like this. You can easily create similar ones.

12: Scoop the wax much as you would a helping of ice cream. If the wax begins to get hard, run some hot water over the scoop to heat it before using.

◄ Unless you are a very fast scooper, you may have to reheat the wax over a low flame, as you work, to maintain the right oatmeal consistency.

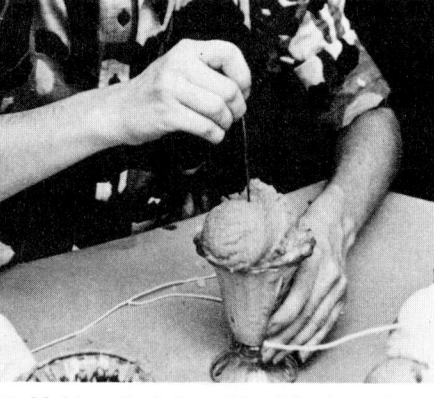

13: Making shaft for wick with piece of wire heated at one end. You can add wick and then put on cherry off-center, or place cherry first and pierce for wick.

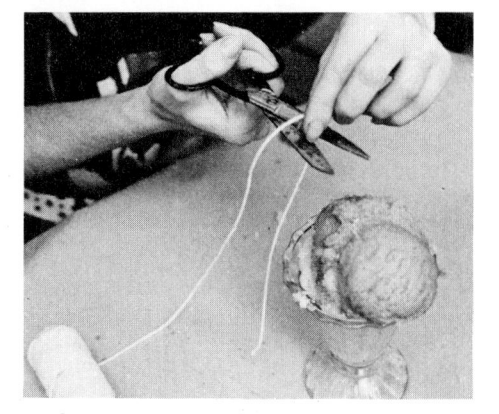

14: Cutting some wick to apply to candle. If you have difficulty inserting it, dip it in some melted wax and then cool it in the refrigerator. This will stiffen it.

Confectionary candles capture the warmth and charm of turn-of-the-century ice-cream parlors. Bring a little of that whimsy to your home by making your own.

photograph 12); a double boiler; a saucepan for each color; a spoon; a suitable glass container; an ice-cream scoop; an eggbeater; a pastry tube (optional) for applying "whipped cream"; a cupful of red wax; a melon-ball scoop; an ice pick or length of wire hanger; and about a foot of wick.

In double boiler, heat wax for the "ice cream" for the inside of the glass. Pour the melted wax into the pan, let it cool. When it is the consistency of oatmeal, stir it and spoon it into the glass container.

Heat wax for the scoops. When it is of oatmeal consistency, pile two or three scoopfuls, in the same or varying colors, onto the wax in the glass.

As described on page 338, whip some white wax with an eggbeater, and pour it over the "ice cream." Or you can use a cake-decorating tube, as I did, to apply the whipped wax as shown in the photograph at right.

For the cherry, carve a melon scoopful of red wax, and set it at the top.

Make a hole for the wick with a heated ice pick or piece of hanger wire (photograph 13), and insert the wick. Apply a little liquid wax around the wick at the opening to seal it.

This elaborate sundae candle is not hard to make. Put whipped wax in pastry tube (available at supermarkets) to make fancy "whipped cream." Or pour on whipped wax.

337

## Carving and Molding
# Molded candles

¢ ⊠ 🚶 🐑

A great variety of containers can be used as molds for making wax candles—milk and cream cartons, containers of plastic, plaster, glass, metal, or ceramic, and almost anything you can improvise. Some candles remain in their molds, such as the soda-pop candle on this page and the candle being made in figure A on the opposite page. Others, such as those made in the metal molds shown in photograph 17, are cast in the containers and are removed as soon as the wax has solidified.

It should be mentioned at this point that if you become really interested in candlemaking as a permanent hobby, you should invest in a dripless and seamless aluminum or stainless-steel pitcher. This is the most important implement in home candlemaking. Although you can improvise with an old coffeepot (see figure A), a pitcher is safer, and it is perfect for pouring or ladeling molten wax into molds. Also, you may want to buy the type of crockery pot that has built-in, unexposed electric elements. This kind of pot is an ideal container for melting wax and is more convenient and even safer than a double boiler.

### Soda-Pop Candle
This is another confectionary-type candle, but it is included here because it is cast in a mold, and the techniques used to make it are the same as those used for other molded candles.

15: Add stearic-acid granules if you are working with unrefined paraffin. Add 20 percent by weight, or follow directions on the container for correct amount.

16: Spoon on the whipped wax after the colored wax in the glass has solidified. A little overflow will make the glass of soda look even more realistic.

Materials you will need are a 10-ounce soda glass, as shown; enough wax to fill the glass; coloring to suit your preference; a cupful of uncolored wax for whipping; an eggbeater or electric blender; an ice pick or short length of wire hanger; about a foot of wick; a short plastic drinking straw.

Melt the wax for filling the glass, and add coloring. Keep in mind that wax tends to lighten in color as it hardens. Test the color your liquid wax will be when it hardens by pouring a drop of it in a basin of cool water. The drop will immediately solidify and reveal its final color.

Allow 15 minutes for the wax to cool. When it has cooled pour it into the glass up to about an inch of the rim.

While this is hardening, prepare some whipped wax, which can be made as easily as whipped cream. Simply pour a cupful of uncolored melted wax into a bowl or pan. Wait until a skim forms on the surface, and then beat with an eggbeater until frothy. For whiteness, add, while whipping 2 or 3 tablespoons of stearic-acid. If you don't like the idea of beating by hand, you can use an electric mixer or blender, but they are a little more difficult to clean. Wax-covered utensils can be heated in a 150-degree oven and wiped clean.

*Mickey Edelman is the president of Aristocrat Candle Corporation of Staten Island, N.Y. He founded the company after having been a candle salesman and having developed new ideas in candle design and production. He has an affinity for unusual candles and specializes in the confectionary kind.*

Only the burning flame gives this creation away as something other than a cool and tempting glass of soda.

When the wax in the glass has solidified, spoon on the whipped wax (photograph 16), and insert the straw. Wait about two or three hours, to make sure the wax has set sufficiently; then make a hole for the wick with a heated ice pick or wire, and insert the wick.

### Professional-Type Molds

Tin and stainless-steel molds, such as those shown in photograph 17, are what professional candlemakers use. They are available in a variety of sizes and shapes for making all kinds of candles and are sold at hobby shops or can be ordered from a number of manufacturers.

To make a candle in a professional-type mold, you will need—in addition to the blocks of wax, wick, melting and pouring containers, and color and scent additives (optional) mentioned in previous projects—a candy thermometer; a tin or steel mold the shape and size of your choice; a spray can of silicone candle-mold release; plastic putty or very sticky and heavy adhesive tape; a pencil or small piece of heavy wire. Anything that will seal the hole at the bottom of the mold without leaking, and is removable, can be used instead of the putty or tape. All of these, with the possible exception

17: These steel and tin molds are only a small sampling of the many shapes and sizes available. Never use molds made of copper. They can stain the wax.

of the candy thermometer, are available at craft or hobby shops. Some hobby shops may have the thermometers, but if not, they can be purchased at any store that sells housewares or baking utensils. Follow these step-by-step instructions to make a candle in any standard mold:

Fill the mold to the brim with water (hold your finger over the wick hole at the bottom), and empty it into the heating container. This will give you an indication of the level of melted wax you will need to fill the mold. Be sure to dry both container and mold before adding wax.

Heat the wax, and prepare the mold while you wait for the wax to melt.

Spray the inside of the mold with the silicone mold release. This will ensure easy removal of the candle, once it has set.

Thread the wicking through the hole in the bottom of the mold (photograph 18, page 340), and extend it well beyond the mouth of the mold at the other end. Knot it at the base end so it cannot slip through the hole.

Figure A: Glass jars or bowls can be used as molds and containers for candles. The technique, with this kind of container, is to tie some wick onto the wick of a small votive candle. Insert this candle, with its extended wick, into container. Hold wick upright, or secure it as shown in photograph 20 on page 340. Pour wax; allow to set. Add more wax, as needed, according to directions for metal-molded candle. Clip off excess wick. Alternate method is to follow this procedure, but to use a wick fastener (photograph 21, page 340) instead of a votive candle.

To make candle at right, add various-color wax cubes to mold; then pour melted wax. For candle at left, use gelatin mold.

339

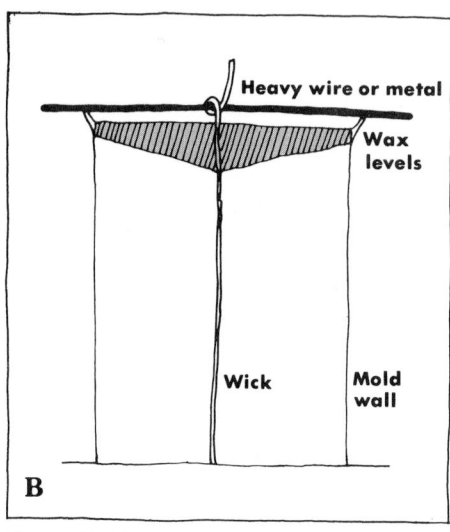

Figure B: This diagram shows a side view of a mold, with wax, wick, and wire in place. The shaded area represents the contraction of the wax as it cools. It also represents the new liquid wax that must be added after each cooling period, until the center of the candle is solid and the top is relatively flat.

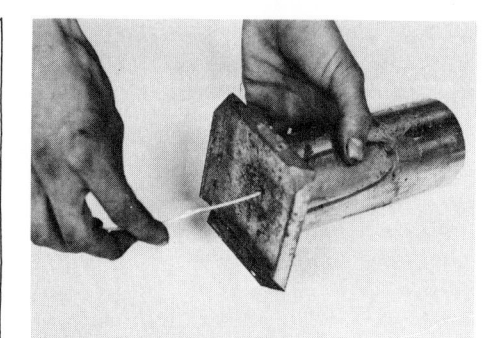

18: Wick for molded candle is threaded through hole in bottom of mold (see instructions on page 339). Before knotting wick, be sure it extends through mold and about 6 inches beyond mouth, to provide enough to tie around wire.

19: Plastic putty is ideal for sealing the hole and the knotted wick. It holds tightly, but can be removed easily when wax has set. Floral clay or heavy and very sticky adhesive tape will work almost as well as the plastic putty.

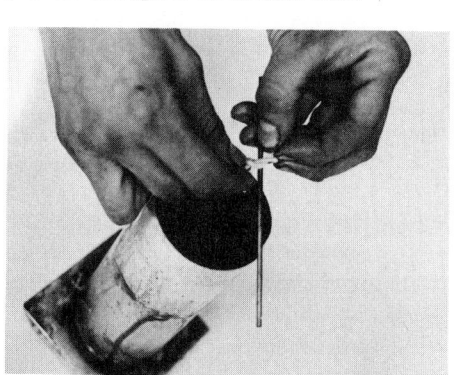

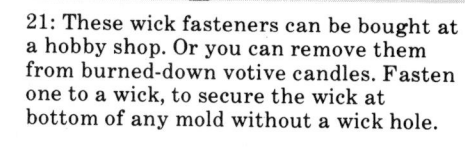

20: Use heavy wire, as shown, a pencil, or a wood stick to hold the wick upright while you pour the melted wax. Rest the wire on the mold; center it, and tie the wick tightly to the wire.

21: These wick fasteners can be bought at a hobby shop. Or you can remove them from burned-down votive candles. Fasten one to a wick, to secure the wick at bottom of any mold without a wick hole.

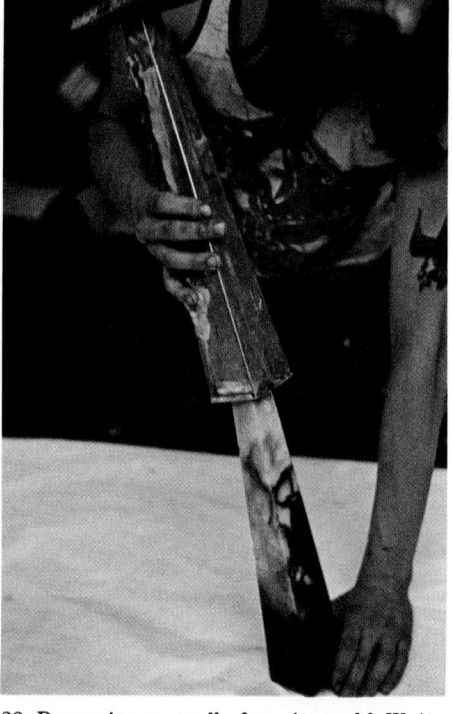

22: Removing a candle from its mold. Wait at least eight hours for wax molecules to set before attempting this final step.

Apply whatever sealer you choose to the hole and wick (photograph 19).

Pull the wick taut; wrap it around a pencil or piece of heavy wire at the mold opening, and tie it (photograph 20). Rest the wire or pencil on the mold, and center the wick as shown in figure B. The mold is now ready.

Set the thermometer in the pouring container (steel pitcher or coffeepot); pour in the melted wax, and let it cool to the ideal pouring temperature (190 to 195 degrees Fahrenheit).

Pour a little wax to cover the bottom of the mold, and let it set for five minutes. This will seal off the wick opening and lessen the chances of any leaks due to the pressure of the liquid wax.

Fill the rest of the mold to about half an inch of the rim. Pour down the center to avoid stripping the silicone coating on the mold walls. When the wax has solidified (about an hour), make an opening down the center with a spoon handle. There will already be a center cavity because of the contraction of the wax as it solidified. Refill this cavity with wax, and let cool. Repeat this procedure once or twice more until a cavity does not reappear. Let the wax set for at least eight hours.

Roll the mold in your hand, pressing lightly, and upend it. The candle should slide out easily (photograph 22). If it does not, run some warm water over the outside of the mold, and try again.

When you have removed the candle from its mold, cut off the excess wick at both ends. What was at the top of the mold will be the bottom of your candle, and vice versa. For a smooth, high-gloss finish, rub the candle a little with an old nylon stocking.

# Carving and Molding
# Wild-flower candles

There are many ways to decorate plain candles that you have made or have purchased. They can be carved, painted, stenciled, decoupaged, or appliqued with small pieces of cast or carved wax. Many of the craft techniques described in these volumes can be applied to decorating candles. Although it is easy to get carried away, it is wise to exercise restraint; an unadorned candle is attractive in itself, and any applied decoration should not detract from its intrinsic beauty.

One of the nicest ways to decorate candles is to use natural materials, such as dried wild flowers, weeds, or ferns, as shown in the color photograph, right. Buttercups, violets, hay, and other small-scale, easily dried flowers or grasses are suitable. Gather these from your garden or house plants (photograph 23), and dry them in one of the commercially prepared products designed for this purpose, such as silica gel (available at garden centers). Follow the directions for drying, or refer to the entry "Dried Flowers."

To make candles like those shown in the color photograph, you will need—in addition to the candles, wild flowers, and drying material mentioned above—some pieces of brown wrapping paper, an iron, a small amount of paraffin or household wax that will have no color added to it, a small saucepan, a glass container large enough to contain wax to be melted, and a large artist's brush (see photograph 24). Follow these simple step-by-step instructions to decorate a candle with dried flowers:

Place the dried flowers or ferns you have selected between two pieces of brown wrapping paper, and press, using a dry iron set at low heat. Iron on an ironing board, or use a hard surface, such as stiff cardboard.

Place glass container into saucepan containing about ½-inch of water. Add wax to glass container and bring water to boil. Melt wax until liquid and keep liquid throughout process.

Position flower on candle and quickly paint hot wax over entire flower. A thin coat is sufficient, but repeat the procedure, if necessary, until the flowers are completely covered and firmly sealed to the candle.

These candles are not suited to being burned all the way down. However, if they are, there is no danger of the dried flowers catching fire. They will only become hot and curl up.

For related projects and crafts, see the entries "Carving," "Casting," "Decoupage," "Dried Flowers," "Molds," "Pressed Flowers," "Stenciling," and "Wild Flowers and Weeds."

*Arlene Hayden, a graduate of the Philadelphia College of Art, is an editorial designer for* Ladies' Home Journal *and a free-lance designer for* American Home Crafts *magazine. She makes candles as a hobby and, while spending time on her parents' farm, got the idea of decorating candles with dried flowers.*

23: If you are an apartment dweller, your potted plants can be a good source of material to dry and apply to plain candles. This Boston fern will not suffer from giving up a few fronds.

24. This candle has had liquid wax brushed on it after dried fern fronds were positioned in place. Here, Miss Hayden gives final touches to seal them to the candle.

Dried specimens of growing things make tasteful, appealing candle decorations.

# New Seats for Chairs

Replacing the woven seat of an elegant old chair seems an impossible home project to many people, I guess. But it isn't. In fact, it really isn't difficult at all. I've taught dozens of people, maybe hundreds, to "bottom" their own chairs. The three projects on the next eight pages will show you, step-by-step, how to weave chair seats of cane, splints, or rush.

The history of chair-seat weaving is obscured in the mists of antiquity. Strips of natural materials like rush, cane, and wooden splints were woven into ground mats many thousands of years ago, archaeologists say. Then came baskets, and I'm sure some prehistoric citizen turned one of them over and sat on it—a kind of woven seat, right? Perhaps someone made a frame of sticks and wove a seat across them. No one knows for sure.

In recent history, woven seats have enjoyed continuous popularity for several hundred years. Sheraton and Chippendale and their many imitators often used rush for seats in their beautiful chairs. In the Victorian Era, people loved the light, crisp look of woven cane. And, of course, country folks have always been partial to hickory and ash splints for the seats of their handmade chairs.

The result is that there are a lot of old chairs around with woven seats that have been broken out or caved in, so you have a great opportunity if you learn how to reweave them.

*Warren Bausert is an expert craftsman who has had 20 years of professional experience in caning and reweaving seats for chairs. He is the owner of the Eli Caning Shop in Centereach, N.Y.*

### Defining Cane, Splints, and Rush

Many people are not clear as to just what cane, splints, and rush are. Cane comes from the outer bark of a certain type of palm tree. It is cut into strips, 1/16- to 3/16-inch wide, and sold in hanks of 1,000 feet—enough to do four chairs. The cost of a hank will vary depending on the width and where you buy it.

Splints are simply long, extremely thin strips of wood—traditionally ash or hickory, but now including wood from the same palm that produces cane. Splints are sold by the one-chair bundle.

Rush is made from the common cattail plant, which has leaves up to 7 feet long. The cattail leaves are gathered in August after the plants are full-grown but before the seed heads start to turn brown. The leaves are seasoned under carefully controlled light, temperature, and humidity conditions so that, as they dry, they do not become too brittle. Then they are twisted into strands. In addition to natural rush, there is a type made of kraft paper which looks very much like the real thing. Rush is sold by the pound; it takes 2 to 3 pounds to do one chair.

### Tools and Materials

Cane, splints, and rush are available from the same sources, although natural rush and splints are often hard to find. Write to Mr. Bausert or try local craft supply houses. Some department stores carry seat-weaving materials. And there are mail order supply houses which often advertise in craft magazines.

Tools you'll need are not unusual: scissors (or shears), tack hammer, tack puller, razor blade, knife, a fine wood rasp, a pan for soaking material, a few spring-type clothespins to clamp loose strands, some old cloth for dampening material, and a narrow, blunt piece of metal for poking and weaving strands. You will also find some special tools that you will need for specific projects mentioned in the project discussion.

The author wove the new cane seat on this attractive maple-and-mahogany chair in a couple of hours. The materials for the job cost about one dollar.

## Furniture and Refinishing
# Weaving a splint seat for a chair $ 🗙 👫 🧵

A splint seat is generally considered appropriate for a chair of simple folk design like the traditional mule-ear chair. Any chair with round rails and stretchers, however, is a candidate for a splint seat.

The splints used for chair seats are usually made from very thin strips of ash or hickory wood, split into strands that are ½-inch, ⅝-inch, or ¾-inch wide. Since lengths vary, splints are sold by the pound or by the bundle. One bundle or 1 pound is enough to bottom an average chair with a seat 16 inches wide. There are other types of splint besides ash and hickory. Flat reed splints are often used instead. Two wider forms of splints, known as flat fiber reed and wide binding cane, can be used for outdoor furniture and certain more sophisticated styles. Whatever the type of splints used, they are all woven in the same way.

Basically, weaving a chair seat is like weaving anything else. You lay down parallel strands, called the warp, in one direction, and insert other strands, called the weft, over and under the warp strands at right angles. Although warp strands may be laid from the front of the chair to the back, in my experience it is easier to lay the warp from side to side. The result should be the same in either case.

Before starting this project, make sure the frame of the chair is in good shape. Remove all old tacks and nails, sand out the scratches, repair any breaks, and apply a new finish, if necessary.

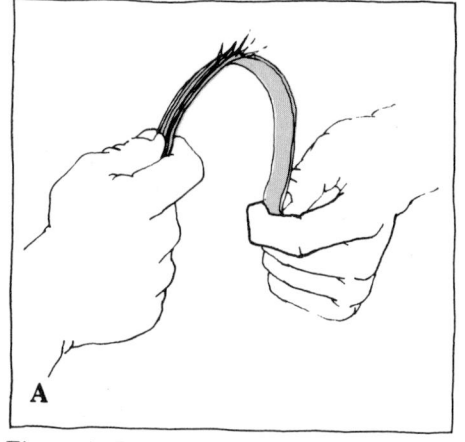

Figure A: Bend each strand of splint, to determine which side should face out. Splinters indicate the wrong side.

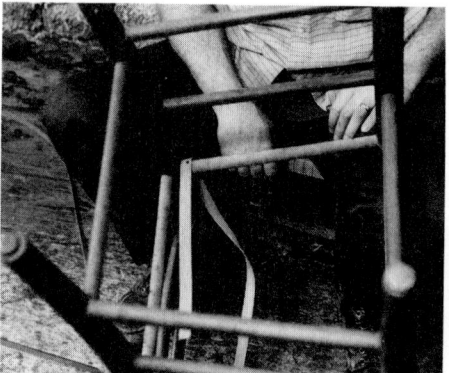

1: Tack first soaked strand of the warp to underside of seat rail. Pull the warper, as these strands are called, over rail and across to opposite rail.

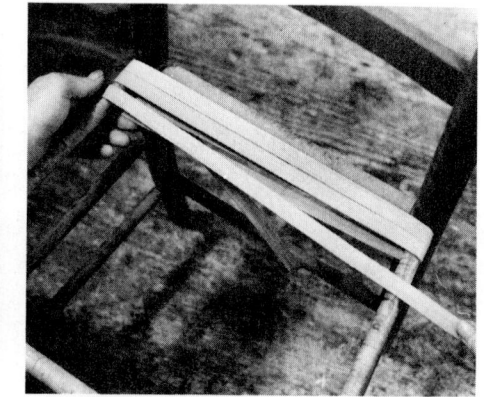

2: Push each strand snugly against the previous strand as you wrap the side rails. Each strand of splint should be soaked 30 minutes or so before using.

3: Use a spring clamp to hold the warper in place while you splice a new strand to it (see figure B). Never splice splints on the top layer or where they turn over the seat rails.

4: When the warp strands are completely laid, clamp the end to a seat rail, but do not cut off the end. Simply tack it, and weave the tail into the seat. Next step is to weave in weft splints.

Strands of splint, woven together, make an attractive and sturdy chair seat. Use this photograph as a weaving pattern as you work on the project.

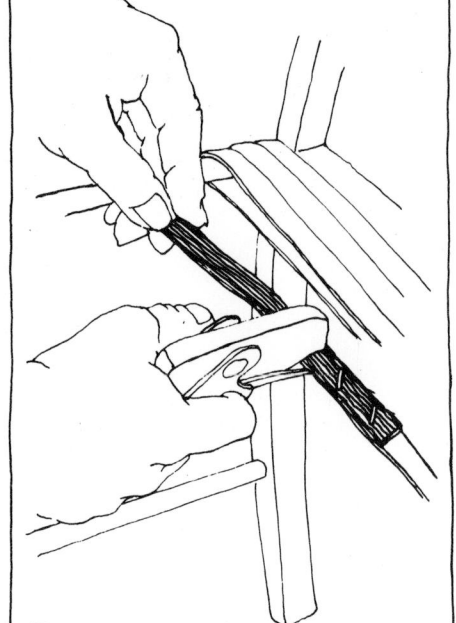

Figure B: Splice the short strands of splint together by overlapping and stapling them as you weave. Splices must fall under seat, where they won't show.

Soak a few splints in water for about 30 minutes, to make them soft and pliable. Coil them for soaking with the nonsplintering side (figure A) facing out. As you remove one splint, put another in to soak, so you will always have a workable supply on hand. Since the strands are comparatively short, you will have to splice each new one to the last strand. A stapler splices well (see figure B), but you can also join splints by notching the edges of both strands and then wrapping them with stout string while they are overlapped. Hide the splices by making them on the bottom layer of splints.

To lay the warp, wrap the strands from side rail to side rail. Start by tacking the first strand (called a warper) to the underside of a rail, leaving four inches or more behind. Bring the warper over the rail, across, and down around the opposite rail. Continue wrapping until the entire seat area is filled. Photographs 1 through 4 show the process of laying the warp. At the finish, clamp the final strand until you have tacked it under the seat rail. Leave about four inches of splint beyond the tack, to be woven into the seat. The seat shown in the photographs took six warpers, spliced together; but seats and splints vary.

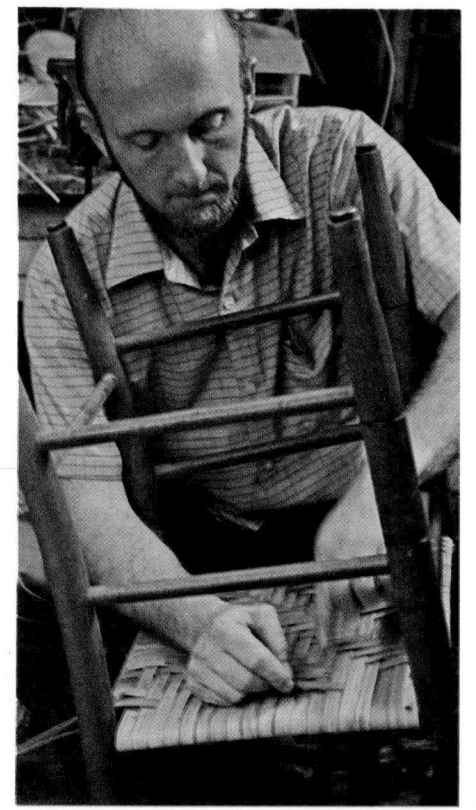

At age 14, the author learned to weave cane, splints, and rush from his father. Now he is teaching a fourth generation of Bauserts this family enterprise.

Herringbone: 1st row is under 1, over 3, under 3, etc.; 2nd row, under 2, over 3, under 3, etc.; 3rd row, under 3, over 3, under 3, etc.; 4th row, over 1, under 3, over 3, etc.; 5th row, over 2, under 3, over 3, etc.

The next step is to weave splints across the warpers at right angles. If the seat were a square or a rectangle, this would be a simple matter, but few seats are. Most are wider in front than in back, so it takes more splints to cover the front rail than the back one. For example, the chair in these photographs required 20 splints across the back rail and 24 across the front. So before you start weaving, do a little measuring.

Subtract the length of the back rail from the length of the front rail, and divide the difference in half. Measure in from each end of the front rail by that amount, and make a pencil mark. The area between the pencil marks and the ends of the back rail is a rectangle, and you can weave normally in that area. But outside the pencil marks, there are two triangles, which also must be woven. Start with the right side first.

Take a short strand of splint, round off one end, and weave it through the warpers at the right end of the front rail. Go under one warper, over three, under three, over three, and so on until you reach the side rail (not the back). Keep it parallel to the line between back corner and pencil mark. Start a second strand next to it, but go under two warpers first and then over three, under three, across the seat. Keep adding short splints until you have filled in up to the pencil mark. It usually requires two or three short splints to fill a corner (see photograph 5). Now turn the chair over, and weave the ends of the filler splints into the bottom warp, continuing with the same pattern you used for the filler strands in the top warp. When this is complete, tuck the loose ends, top and bottom, into the center of the seat and tack each strand to the underside of the chair rail (see photograph 7).

Take a full length of splint, and weave it from the pencil mark to the end

5: Weave short splints into front corner first, to square up the rest of the cross-woven strands. This is done because seat is wider at the front than at the back.

6: Underside of chair seat shows how the short corner splints are woven across the bottom and then their ends are buried between the top and the bottom strands.

7: Tack all short filler strands to the underside of front rail, to hold them in place. Only the first and the last full-length strands need to be tacked.

8: Weave full-length strands of splint across seat and around back rail. Weave bottom as you did the top. Keep each strand tight against preceding strand.

9: Use a small knife or similar tool to help slip weaving strand between warpers as the seat becomes tight near the finish. End of last strand tucks inside.

of the back rail, keeping it tight against the filler strand. Carefully study the weaving pattern (see color photograph on page 345) before starting to weave. It is three under, three over, continued across, with each new strand starting one warper over. Round off the leading end of each splint to make weaving easier.

After weaving the first strand of splint across to the back rail, tack the other end to the underside of the front rail alongside the filler strands. Bring the first strand around the back rail, and weave it across the bottom in the same pattern. Fill in the entire seat area this way, joining strands on the bottom layer as necessary. When you reach the pencil mark at the other end of the front rail, tuck the end of the strand inside, tack it down, and insert two or three short filler strands, as in the beginning.

The last step is to apply finish to the splint seat. It can be stained like ordinary wood if you want it to match the wood of the chair. Trim off all loose strands first. One popular finish is a mixture of half linseed oil, half turpentine. Let it soak in, then wipe the seat dry. Protect it with shellac or, instead, use any clear, penetrating sealer.

11: In the first step, lay cane from center hole in back rail to center hole in front. Tapered pegs hold cane taut. Reserve back corner hole for diagonals.

12: Tie off cane ends underneath the rails, using this simple knot. After the cane dries, the knot will hold tightly.

13: Complete the vertical cane on the other side of the seat, pegging the ends. The short strands on each side serve to square up pattern in the curved area.

14: Second step starts with horizontal strand laid over vertical strands across back. Don't use corner holes.

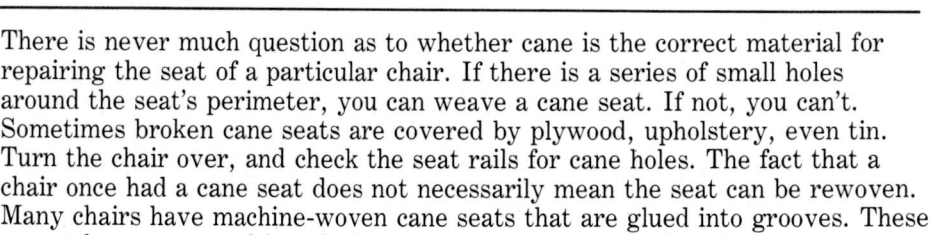

10: To soften cane, soak it for 10 to 20 minutes in lukewarm water. Do not over-soak; that could discolor the cane and make it more brittle when it dries.

**Furniture and Refinishing**
# Recaning a chair seat    $ ⏱ 🚶 🧵

There is never much question as to whether cane is the correct material for repairing the seat of a particular chair. If there is a series of small holes around the seat's perimeter, you can weave a cane seat. If not, you can't. Sometimes broken cane seats are covered by plywood, upholstery, even tin. Turn the chair over, and check the seat rails for cane holes. The fact that a chair once had a cane seat does not necessarily mean the seat can be rewoven. Many chairs have machine-woven cane seats that are glued into grooves. These cannot be rewoven, although the seats can be replaced. (See the entry on "Finishing and Refinishing.")

Before you start to recane, get the chair into shape. Remove any seat covering the caning area, repair breaks, cut away any old cane left, clean out the cane holes, and refinish the chair if necessary.

Cane is usually sold in hanks or bunches of about 1,000 feet, which is enough to do four average chair seats. It comes in six sizes, according to strand width. What is called common is the widest cane and is suitable for 5/16-inch cane holes that are about an inch apart. Carriage cane is the thinnest size and is suitable for ⅛-inch holes that are ⅜ inch apart. The four in-between sizes are superfine, fine-fine, fine, and medium. It's a good idea to show the seller a sample of the old cane if you have one. You will also need five or six tapered pegs to hold the cane in place while you work.

To make the cane workable, soak it in lukewarm water for 10 to 20 minutes. Before using a strand, wipe it dry, so the water won't make the wood of the rail swell and decrease the size of the cane holes.

There is a seven-step sequence to weaving a cane seat. You first lace the cane vertically, from rear seat rail to front seat rail. Second, lace the cane horizontally. Third, weave the cane diagonally. Fourth, lay down a second vertical layer. Fifth, weave a second horizontal layer. Sixth, weave a second diagonal layer. Seventh, lace binder cane over the holes. Tie off cane ends beneath the rails as you go (photograph 12).

Handwoven cane chair seat has even, octagonal holes when it is done correctly.
Use this photograph as a pattern to check your work.

15: Vertical and horizontal canes have
been laid and squared up, completing
steps one and two. Don't pull too tight.

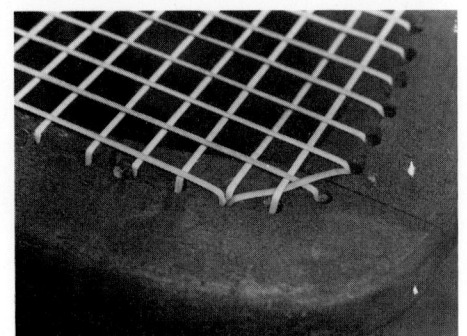

16: In the third step, start the first
diagonal at right front corner of the
seat. These weavers go under all vertical
canes, over horizontal ones.

17: Note that two of these diagonal
weavers go into the same hole. This is
sometimes necessary in curved part of
seat rails, to maintain the star pattern.

18: In the fourth step, lay second course
of vertical cane over all strands and
to right of previous vertical strands.

Step one: Start vertical strands of cane from center hole in back rail to
center hole in front rail. Count the holes to be sure. If there is an even
number of holes, start with a hole nearest the center. Push about 4 inches
of cane through back center hole, and hold it with a wooden peg. Pull cane
across and down through the front center hole, making sure the smooth side of
the cane faces up. Bring the end of the cane along the underside of the front
rail and up through the next hole. Then go across seat to the next hole in
the back rail and down through. Then over to the next hole, up through it,
across to the front rail, and down through the next hole there. Continue
lacing the cane this way until half of the seat is covered (photograph 11).
Then cover the other half the same way. Don't pull the cane too tight; it
will shrink as it dries. Knot ends as in photograph 12.

Step two: Lace the horizontal strands across from side rail to side rail the
same way. These strands lie on top of the vertical ones (photograph 15).

Step three: Weave the first diagonal strands, starting at the right front
corner (photograph 16), over horizontal strands and under vertical strands.
To maintain six-pointed star pattern, you may need to put two strands through
the same hole, because of curvature of side rails (photograph 17).

Step four: Lay a second course of vertical cane over the work thus far,
using the same holes as for the first course (photograph 18). This course is
not woven in. Lay cane to the right of the original vertical strands.

Step five: Weave in a second course of horizontal strands (photograph 19,
page 350), using the same holes as the first course. These strands go under
diagonal course and first vertical course, and over second vertical course.
Place them to the rear of horizontal strands laid down in step two.

Step six: Weave in a second course of diagonal strands, going in the opposite
direction from the first diagonal course (photograph 21, page 350). These
weavers always go under all horizontal and over all vertical strands, just the
opposite of the way in which diagonal strands were laid down in step three.

Step seven: Fasten the binder cane around the seat's perimeter (photographs
22 through 24 and figure C) to cover the cane holes. Binder cane is usually
just cane that is one size wider than the cane you use for weaving. Measure
enough to go around.

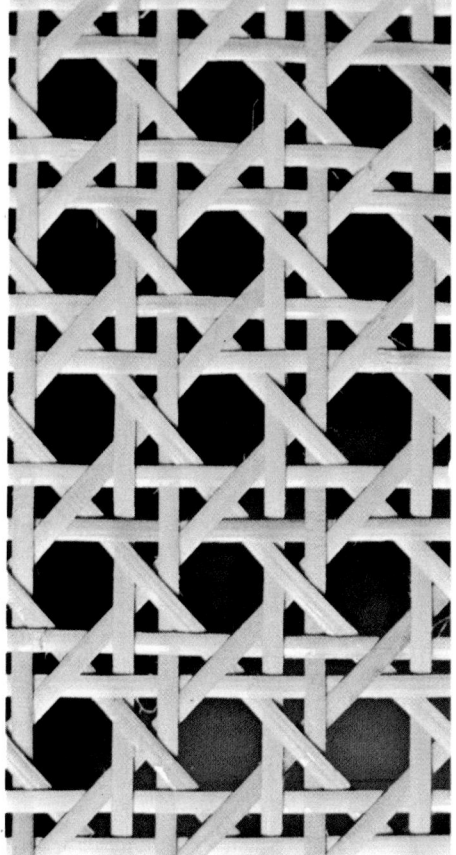

Good-quality cane is easier to weave because it has no splits or rough eyes.

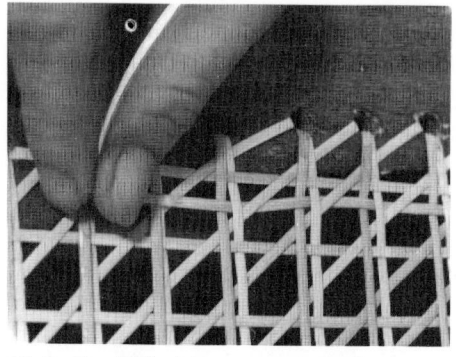

19: In the fifth step, weave second horizontal course across, using the same holes as in step two. Lay these weavers to rear of strands laid in step two.

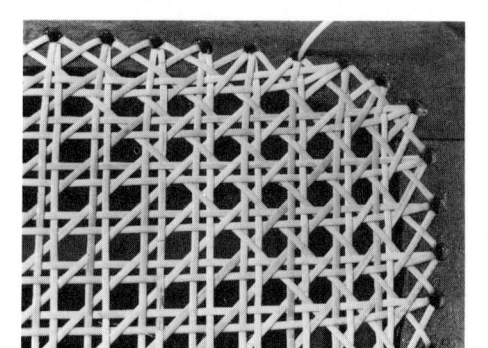

21: In the sixth step, weave a second diagonal strand in the opposite direction from strand in step three. These weavers go under horizontals, over verticals.

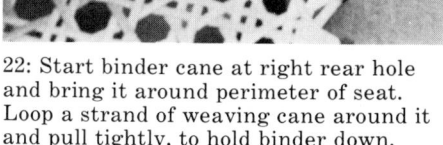

20: In tight areas, use an awl or similar tool to lift cane under which a weaver must pass. Do not pull the cane too tight, as it will shrink as it dries.

22: Start binder cane at right rear hole and bring it around perimeter of seat. Loop a strand of weaving cane around it and pull tightly, to hold binder down.

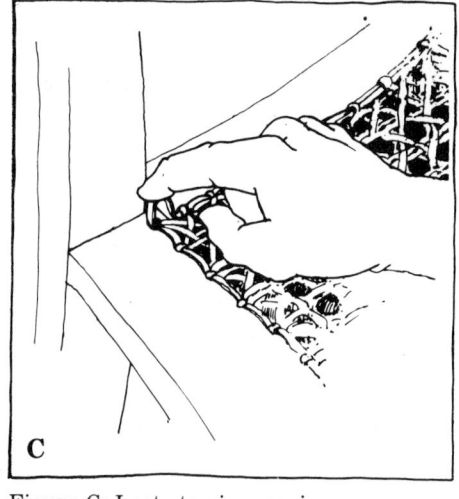

Figure C: Last step in weaving a cane seat is to cover holes and cane ends with binder cane, shiny side up. End of binder is pushed into the starting hole.

Push one end of the binder cane into the corner hole at the right rear corner (photograph 22), and lay out the rest along the back edge of the cane. Select a long strand of weaving cane, and pull all but 4 inches through the hole next to one where binder started. Loop end of weaving cane around binder, and pull it through the same hole, tying the binder down. Then bring the long end of the cane up through the next hole, over the binder, and back down through the same hole. Continue this with each hole until you have tied the binder down all the way around. Tuck the end of the binder into the same hole where you started (figure C).

23: To turn a square corner with binder cane, push end of tied strand through corner hole; tie it off; then start new strand of binder, as in the beginning.

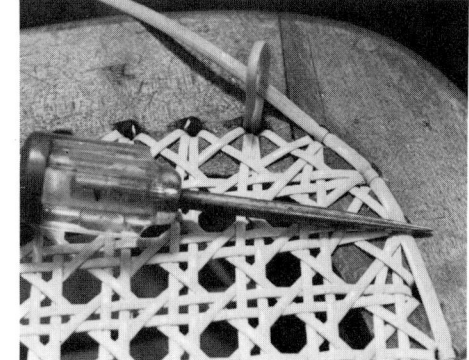

24: Work binder cane around the curved front corner of the chair seat. Keep cane damp and pliable to prevent breaking. An awl helps open up holes.

## Furniture and Refinishing
# Making a rush chair seat

A fiber-rush seat is quite easy to make, once you learn to weave your way around. Essentially, it is a matter of taking the rush cord from rail to rail, laying each strand close to the preceding one, until the rails are filled. The rush cord is looped at each corner, under and over one rail and then under and over the rail at right angles to it. Each trip the cord makes around all four corners of the seat is called a bout.

The cord used for this project is fiber rush, which is not the same as real rush. Fiber rush is made of strong kraft paper, twisted into continuous strands. Real rush is made by twisting the leaves of the cattail plant as you weave. I only use real rush when I am restoring a rare antique chair.

This beautifully woven rush seat enhances the style of an antique ladderback chair. The art of rushing is quite easy to learn.

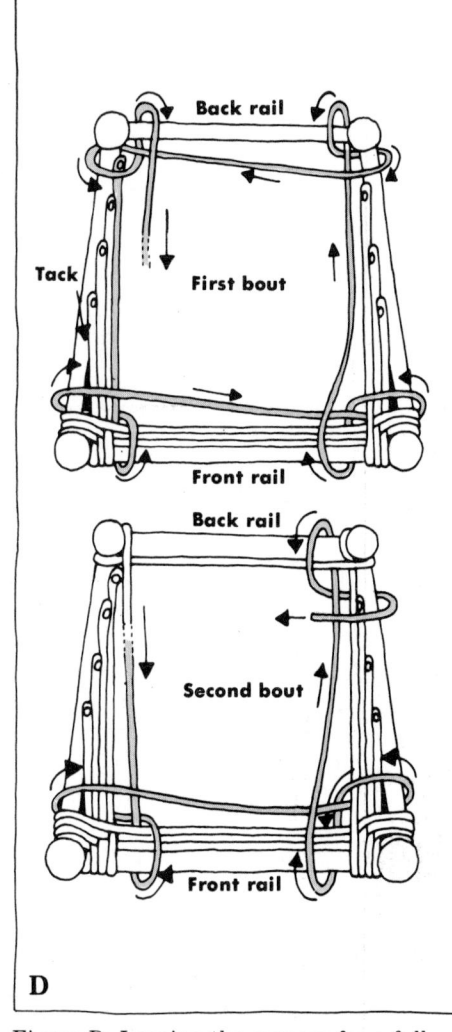

Figure D: Looping the corners for a full bout is simple. On the next round (called a bout), you simply repeat the first. Continue weaving this same pattern until the chair seat is filled.

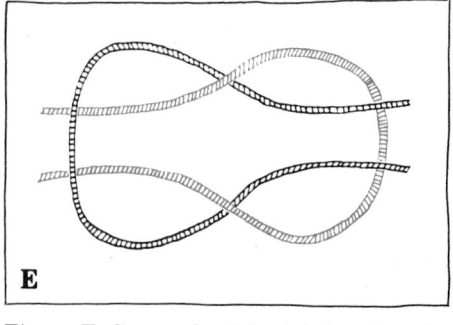

Figure E: Square knot for joining strands of fiber rush is done always on underside of seat, where knot won't show. Natural rush is simply twisted together.

Fiber rush is sold by the reel or by the pound. Two pounds will do an average small seat, 3 pounds a large one. Fiber rush comes in different diameters: 3/32, 4/32, 5/32, and 6/32 inch. The two largest sizes are most commonly used, because they fill in more seat area with less work. Some people think the 6/32-inch size looks more like real rush. Fiber rush does not have to be soaked before it is woven.

The first step is to prepare the chair for its new seat. Cut away the old seat and remove any tacks or nails you find. Fill any dents and cracks, repair anything broken, and refinish as needed.

### Squaring up the seat

Now you are ready to start weaving the rush cord. If the seat is rectangular or square, you can start right in weaving full bouts. But if the seat is wider at the front than at the back, as most seats are, you have to fill in the front corners to square up the seat. It is very important that all cords cross the rails at right angles; otherwise, there will be a large gap in the center. This means that if it takes 60 cords to fill the back rail, it will take more than 60 to fill the front rail. So you have to add extra filler cords up front. To determine how much filling you need to do, simply measure the front and back rails. Using half the difference between their lengths, measure in from each end of the front rail. Make

25: Start at left front corner, and tack short strand of rush to side rail. Bring it under front rail; loop over the top and under the side rail, as shown. Then take it under opposite side rail and tack.

26: Second cord is tacked alongside the first and brought across the seat the same way. Tack each of these short cords to the opposite rail. It may take a dozen or so to square off the opening.

pencil marks at these spots. Everything outside these marks must be filled.

The procedure for filling in the corners is clearly shown in photographs 25, 26, and 27. (Directions are given as if you were facing the chair.) Start by tacking one end of a short piece of rush cord inside the left side rail. Bring it under the front rail and then over. Now bring it under the left side rail and over. Then bring the cord across, under the right side rail and over it. Bring it under the front rail next, then over it. Tack the cord to the right side rail directly across from where you tacked it to the left side rail. Cut off the extra cord.

Continue laying these short filler cords until the front rail is covered from the ends to the pencil marks. Remember that each time the rush cord comes over a rail, it crosses all the standing cords before going under the rail at right angles to it.

Now you are ready to weave the first full bout, as shown in figure D. Cut off about 50 feet of rush cord. Some rush weavers use longer strands, but the more you cut off, the more you have to keep pulling through. You will attach the next strand with a square knot, as shown in figure E. Tack one end of the cord to the left side rail, just behind the last filler cord, and weave it just as you did the fillers. But, instead of tacking it to the right side rail, continue through to the back rail and around, looping each corner following the pattern shown in figure D.

Continue weaving around like this for 12 to 15 bouts. As you weave, push each cord tightly against its neighbor where it turns around the rails. Use a block of wood and a small hammer to compact them snugly against each other.

The next step is to stuff the seat. The four triangular pockets must be stuffed separately. You will see the pockets beginning to form between top and bottom layers. Simply stuff newspaper into the corners of each pocket, and continue stuffing as you weave. Or cut four triangles of corrugated cardboard, insert them in the pockets, and weave around them.

Continue weaving until the side rails are completely covered. If the seat is wider than it is deep, the front rails will not be covered yet. Wherever you are at this point, just continue weaving from front to back rail (or vice versa), going between the cross cords in the center, as in figure F. Weave these figure eights across from one side to the other until the front and back rails are filled. Use a block of wood and a hammer to mash cords flat where they cross to fill in better. Bring the cord underneath, and untwist about 4 inches at the end. Apply glue and retwist the cord end into an adjoining cord. To finish the seat, stain it as you wish, and then give it a couple of coats of thin shellac.

For entries on related projects and crafts, see "Antiquing Furniture," "Basketry," "Finishing and Refinishing," "Macrame," "Weaving," "Woodworking."

27: To square up the seat, fill in the corners with short strands of rush. Tack each strand to the side rails at both ends. When corner areas are full, you can weave one strand around continuously.

28: After four full bouts, the seat looks like this, each strand at right angles to front and back rails. The work moves quickly from now on. If you must stop, clamp the rush to keep it tight.

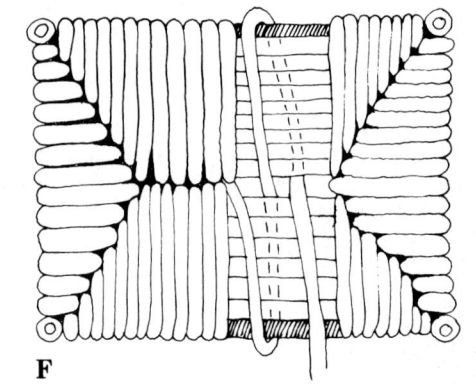

**F**

Figure F: When a seat is wider than it is deep, side rails will be filled before front and back rails are. Fill in by simply weaving figure eights through the center. Mash the rush flat where it crosses, so it will fill in better.

29: The strands of a well-woven rush seat are laid tightly together. Use a hammer and a block of wood to compact them. Finish the seat with shellac.

# CANOEING
## Outdoor Family Challenge

*Stuart James was outdoors editor for* Popular Mechanics *for six years, executive editor of* True *for two years, and is now editor of* Rudder. *He grew up in the outdoors, running a trapline along Neshaminy Creek in southeast Pennsylvania at eight, fishing and hunting at every available moment. He first paddled a canoe at seven. Since then, he figures he has paddled over 1500 miles. He considers work boats the most interesting craft and the canoe the best and most versatile of work boats. His ten-year-old son, Morgan, who had never been in a canoe before, assisted him in the demonstration here.*

Canoeing is a natural activity. Put anyone in a canoe for the first time with a paddle in his hands and he will paddle spontaneously and correctly the first time he dips the paddle into the water. His motions will be a bit clumsy at first—he will dig the paddle in, splash, lean heavily into the stroke, and tilt the canoe to one side. But within an hour he will have adjusted himself to paddling, and by the end of a day the average person—man, woman, even a child—will find he can paddle well. After a few canoe trips, he can be quite expert.

I believe this is one reason why the canoe design has remained virtually unchanged since this Indiancraft was discovered by French explorers who came to North America early in the seventeenth century. Samuel de Champlain never ceased to marvel at the speed and maneuverability of the birch-bark canoe, and he adopted it immediately for his push into the interior. A canoe was, and is, the perfect craft for stream, river, and lake. Construction materials have changed, but the design is the same—there is simply no reason to alter it.

The most popular canoe today is made of aluminum, with fiberglass running a close second. You can still buy canvas-covered wooden canoes, and although they are heavy and expensive and require considerable maintenance care, they have their place in lake running. For river running and general touring, aluminum and fiberglass canoes are superior. They are lighter, maintenance-free, and inexpensive. If a rock tears a hole in either type

The canoe is the only watercraft native to North America. The canoe design we know today was fully developed when the first European explorers arrived on this continent. It is singularly well adapted to inland waters, and although ideally it is managed by two paddlers, it can be handled easily by one ten-year-old paddling from the stern.

of craft, it is easily repaired. (See Canoeing Craftnotes on pages 364 and 365.) If you plan to canoe on a large lake, the canvas-covered wood type is best. It has a deeper keel, higher gunwales, a high, wide bow for taking large waves, and cork sponsons (floats) along the gunwales to improve stability.

### Getting to Know the Craft

Before you take out a canoe, spend a couple of hours with an aluminum or fiberglass model getting to know the craft and its responses.

Safely strapped into life jackets, in shallow, calm water, practice exchanging seats with your partner, rising simultaneously, moving forward and aft in a low crouch, balancing each others weight and motion as you advance. A canoe is a light, buoyant craft, and difficult to balance in if you stand too tall or move quickly and thoughtlessly. However, its buoyancy makes it hard to capsize and impossible to sink as long as it is intact.

Handling a capsize situation is another drill a beginner should practice in shallow water, in part to learn just how hard it is to overturn that seemingly unstable craft, and in part to gain confidence in his ability to handle a capsize should it occur. To capsize the canoe, lean heavily to one side until it tips over. It rarely will completely overturn. More often, paddlers spill into the water and the canoe fills with water but stays upright. Air chambers under the fore and aft decks will keep the water-filled canoe afloat and will support your weight as well. To get underway again, one paddler holds the canoe steady while the other bails with bailer, tin can, hat or hands. Partially bailed, the canoe is guided to shore and emptied. If the canoe does turn upside down, dive and come inside it. You will find it filled with air. Holding to the seats inside, paddle the canoe to shore.

1: Even when filled with water, the capsized canoe is unsinkable and an excellent life raft. It can be paddled even when it is partially submerged.

In safety drill, canoe is capsized in shallow water, above; paddled to shore although filled with water, below.

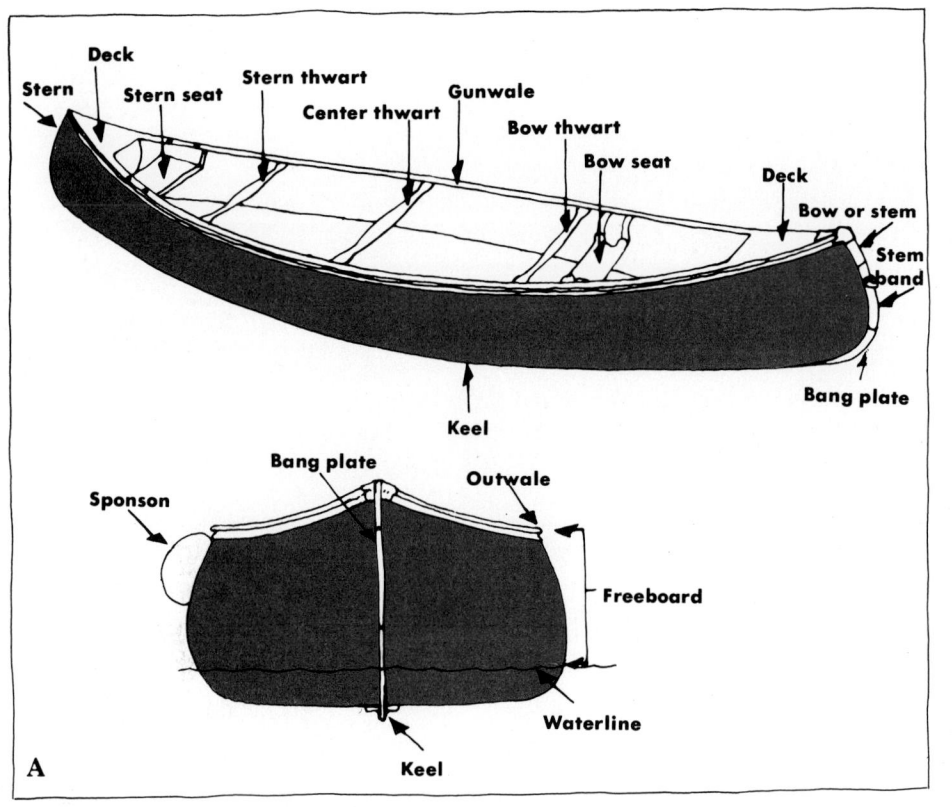

Figure A: This diagram shows the basic canoe. Some of the elements are modified for special work. A lake canoe handles better with a deeper keel; for long passages in open water, it is advisable to have a canoe with high, curving bow and stern and high gunwales. For constant white-water paddling, a wide, flat keel offers protection from rocks. The sponson, a shaped half-round of cork running the length of the canoe just below the gunwales, is optional, but it keeps the craft from capsizing.

## How to Paddle a Canoe

There are two paddling positions in a canoe—bow (front) and stern (back). The stern paddler controls the canoe's direction, sets the pace, and calls instructions to the bow paddler. The more experienced canoeist generally takes the stern seat, the novice or smaller canoeist, the bow.

The bow paddler in a cruising canoe uses the basic power stroke most of the time. This is really doing what comes naturally. Paddling on the right side, you hold the grip of the paddle loosely in the palm of the left hand and grasp the shaft with the right hand. You dip the paddle blade into the water ahead of you, pull it back with the right arm, lift the blade clear of the water, move it forward, and repeat the maneuver. That's all there is to it. You change hands for the left-side power stroke.

The most important part of paddling is to feel comfortable and set a pace that agrees with you. Don't lunge into the strokes or do all your vigorous paddling in the first five minutes. Dip the paddle, stay upright and pull back, keeping the paddle straight and close to the side of the canoe.

Sitting in the rear, the stern paddler adjusts his stroke and pace to the bowman. He uses a variety of strokes, but all are so suited to the control of the craft that he would do them without knowing their names. For straight cruising, he uses the power stroke in unison with the bow paddler, but on the opposite side. If he is getting off course, he applies the J stroke or the steering stroke. The J stroke is merely a forward carry through after the power stroke; this pulls the bow to right or left. The steering stroke (you will hear several names for all these strokes) is simply keeping the blade of the paddle slightly angled during the stroke and holding it for a few seconds at the end of the stroke, like a rudder; this also guides the bow to right or left.

For making an abrupt turn, the stern paddler digs the paddle in at the end of a stroke and pushes down and forward, while the bow paddler executes a wide, sweeping arc that sends the bow around. Again, these are such normal movements that a novice canoeist would do them almost automatically. A common problem with many novices is digging in the paddle just before

2: The bow stroke is a simple movement of dipping the paddle blade toward the bow and pulling straight back without touching the canoe. The body is kept as vertical as possible, with the arms performing most of the work.

3: The J stroke, performed at stern, is particularly useful for adjusting direction when strong bowman overpowers stern paddler in basic cruising stroke. Stern man pulls paddle through stroke, sculls (strokes at an angle) to the right, then pushes forward and holds before the next stroke.

4: The bow rudder stroke is a simple maneuver for pulling the bow to right or left. In the execution, the paddler just reverses the position of the pulling hand on the shank of the paddle to push, dips the blade forward of the bow position, and holds against the canoe's momentum. It is most effective in fast water when the bowman sees a submerged obstacle.

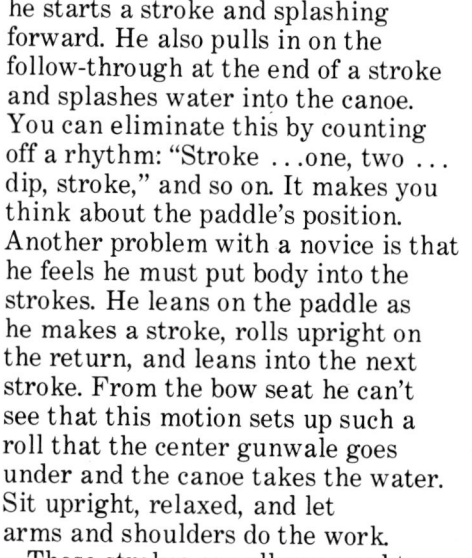

▲ 5: A quarter sweep turns canoe sharply without loss of speed. Paddles—on right, as above, or on left, opposite—are moved in unison through a wide, shallow arc.

6: The stern rudder stroke is strictly a steering maneuver. At the end of a normal cruising stroke, the paddle is held on a diagonal while bow paddler goes through his next stroke. In fast water, this directs the canoe without paddling.

7: The jam stroke stops the canoe dead in the water and brings the bow to right or left. The paddle blade is placed fully into the water at the rear of a stroke, then pushed forward with force.

he starts a stroke and splashing forward. He also pulls in on the follow-through at the end of a stroke and splashes water into the canoe. You can eliminate this by counting off a rhythm: "Stroke ...one, two ... dip, stroke," and so on. It makes you think about the paddle's position. Another problem with a novice is that he feels he must put body into the strokes. He leans on the paddle as he makes a stroke, rolls upright on the return, and leans into the next stroke. From the bow seat he can't see that this motion sets up such a roll that the center gunwale goes under and the canoe takes the water. Sit upright, relaxed, and let arms and shoulders do the work.

These strokes are all you need to know for canoeing in average water on rivers and lakes.

### Selecting a Paddle

The most important thing in selecting a paddle is to get the proper fit. For the stern man, the paddle should reach from floor to forehead; for the bowman, from floor to chin. Quality is not essential for the novice, but make sure you have a spare paddle for each paddler. Ash and maple are the best woods and the quality of the wood and the craftsmanship are important. When you reach the stage where you call a paddle a blade, you are ready to shop for a good one.

10: The bow sweep, which is also called the quarter sweep, is used to swing the bow sharply. When it is used in conjunction with a strong power stroke at the stern, the canoe both turns and gains speed. If the stern man applies the steering stroke or a jam stroke, the turn is tight and abrupt.

## Portaging the Canoe

An 18-foot canoe weighs about 120 pounds. Since the weight is well distributed, it is not difficult to carry (portage) for short distances. When you haul this weight uphill on rough ground, through brush, and over boulders, however, a carry of only a quarter mile can be tiring.

Unless exceptionally strong and used to carrying a canoe, the two-man carry is recommended. With the canoe right side up and one man at each end and on opposite sides, each takes a handhold under the deck and lifts. A variation is the two-man shoulder carry. Some shoulder padding helps—a blanket or a rolled-up jacket will do. The canoe is turned upside down; the stern is lifted and placed on the shoulder of one man. The bowman (opposite side) then lifts it to his shoulder. This carry is particularly good in brush as it raises the canoe above the tops of most bushes you are likely to encounter.

If you are four men travelling with two canoes, you will save energy by making two trips and putting four men on each canoe. An important point about portaging: Allow plenty of time, and make the loads as light as possible. You may read about carrying a gear-packed canoe, but don't do it. You are out for a good time, and if you arrive at the campsite exhausted after a

8: The in-draw stroke is used most often in white water where abrupt changes of direction are necessary. The paddler reaches out with the blade parallel to the canoe, plunges it into the water, and pulls it toward the canoe with as much speed and force as he can muster.

9: With only one paddler, every power stroke swings the bow. So it is necessary to paddle on alternate sides or hold the blade as a rudder after each stroke. If the paddle is held on a diagonal, it keeps the canoe in a straight line and eliminates compensating strokes.

11: A stroke particularly adapted to single-handed paddling is the stern sweep. It swings the bow in a sharp turn without loss of speed or a break in paddling rhythm. This is the same as the quarter sweep, but is a more effective stroke with the bow out of the water.

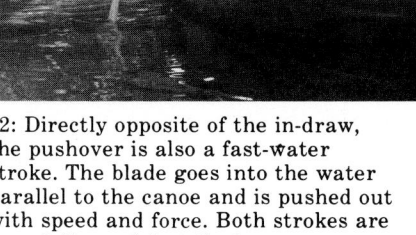

12: Directly opposite of the in-draw, the pushover is also a fast-water stroke. The blade goes into the water parallel to the canoe and is pushed out with speed and force. Both strokes are especially useful at the bow.

14: Paddles have been lashed between the thwarts to form a yoke for the one-man carry. If the shoulders are padded, a canoe can be easily carried this way for surprisingly long distances.

15: The two-man shoulder carry is relatively easy, even with a ten-year-old at one end, although frequent rests are recommended during long portages. Carriers are on opposite sides, for balance.

16: Two-man carry for a short portage or to place the canoe in the water has one man on each side, grasping the bow and stern decks. Not recommended for narrow paths or long distances.

17: Lifting the canoe for a one-man carry is made easier by raising one end and resting it on the branch of a tree. The carrier then crouches into the yoke and lifts the canoe away from the tree.

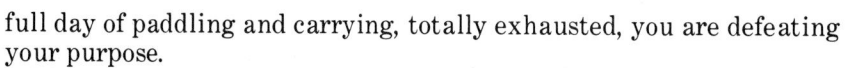

13: Initial step in the one-man carry is lifting the canoe onto the thighs. Then the thwarts are grasped, and in one swinging motion, the craft is lifted overhead and settled on the shoulders, where it is adjusted for balance.

full day of paddling and carrying, totally exhausted, you are defeating your purpose.

The one-man carry for any distance is grueling, but it can be done, and in time (believe it or not) you can almost get used to it. You fashion a yoke by lashing two paddles on the thwarts (photograph 14). I like the yoke to be slightly V-shape, with the blades of the paddles forward. This allows me to move into the yoke and get the canoe in a comfortable position on my shoulders. And with my hands on the paddle blades, I have a controlling leverage for the weight. The prescribed method of getting the canoe onto the shoulders is to lift one side so the bottom is resting against the knees, grasp the thwarts, and lift the canoe onto the thighs. You are now stooping. Reach across and grasp the thwarts on the far side, and roll the canoe onto your shoulder. Grasp both gunwales, and with one movement, lift with both arms at the same time, and duck your head under the canoe. Lower the yoke onto your shoulders, get comfortable, and you are ready to go. If a tree is available, and one ususally is, I just drag the canoe to the base of its trunk and lift the bow end until it can be propped against the lowest limb. I step under the canoe, get comfortable in the yoke, and lift. Then I back away from the tree and am on my way.

The techniques of portaging vary with the terrain and with the distance of the carry. The objective is to move the canoe and supplies overland around an obstacle—and you must adapt your method of accomplishing the task to the nature of the obstacle confronting you.

Lining a canoe is not really a portage, but you will think about it when you first encounter rapids you don't want to run and you don't feel like making a carry, so I will mention it here. Lining is merely tying long lines to the fore and aft thwarts and letting the canoe float down through the rapids while you and your partner, holding the lines on opposite sides of the stream, control its descent. This sounds easy, but it can be tricky if the water is swift. The only way to learn it is to try it. Tracking a canoe is the same maneuver, except that the canoe is pulled upstream through rapids.

## White-Water Canoeing

The ultimate thrill for the canoeist is running white water. This is when his sport moves into the category of soaring or rock climbing or scuba diving and skill is thoroughly tested. There is always the tingling feeling of apprehension as you approach the drop-off for the first run of the day, holding back and standing to survey the rapids and decide on a course. This changes to exhilaration as the canoe picks up speed and plunges into what appears to be a maelstrom. From then on, you are too busy to think much about emotions, but the remembrance of the run is a blend of high excitement, shouting, rushing water, the soul-wrenching crunch when the canoe slammed

Poised before the first drop into a run of white water on Connecticut's Housatonic River, father and son experience the elation and camaraderie that are part of this exciting activity.

into submerged rock, the springboard resilience of the hull as it bounded off unscathed, laughter, controlled panic, a feeling of unfettered joy.

The dangers of white water are real and ever present, but they can be reduced to nearly zero with care and planning. The best way the novice can be introduced to white water is for him to compete in a downriver race for open canoes sponsored by a recognized canoe club. Since the course is planned for open canoes, it will be exciting, but not too dangerous. There will be plenty of canoeists on the river, so you will have company and assistance if needed—and you can follow others and imitate them. If sections of the rapids are difficult, you can be certain the shore will be lined with spectators looking for thrills, and should you capsize and get into trouble, there will be many hands to help you. Hundreds of races are held each spring, when the water is good, high and fast, all over the country.

Special equipment is essential in white water. You should wear a plastic helmet to protect your head, a good life jacket, and tile-setter's kneepads. Footwear is also important, because you will be in and out of the canoe a great deal, hauling it over shallows or freeing it from a cleft in rocks, and the footing will be slippery and uneven. A pair of sturdy, ankle-high work shoes will give you good protection from stone bruises and twisted ankles, and you will be glad to have something solid on your feet when one foot slips between two rocks and you are wrestling with a wild canoe.

Keeping a low profile is vitally important in white water. Both paddlers kneel on the bottom of the canoe. The bowman kneels behind the forward thwart; this frees him from entanglement with the bow seat, raises the bow slightly, and gives him more mobility. The stern man kneels just forward of the stern seat. In these positions both men have their center of gravity below the gunwales, have greater stroking power, and, in the event of trouble, can crouch down into the canoe for more stability. It is always startling to find yourself suddenly going through the rapids stern first; but in most cases when a canoe is clearly out of control, if the paddlers concentrate on the lowest possible profile and on balance, the canoe will go through the rapids unaided or will at least come to rest in a stable enough position so they can regain control and proceed.

All the advanced paddling strokes come into play when a pair of experts are weaving in and around the rocks in a stretch of fast water. The bowman will be using the jam stroke, the bow rudder, the draw stroke, the sweep stroke. The stern man will be backwatering, jamming, drawing in, and pushing out. When two men work well together, there is a lightning-fast, coordinated effort, punctuated by shouts; the paddles flash in and out of the water, flicking to right or left; the canoe, responding, dodges this way and that.

18: Safety equipment is required for white-water canoeing. A life jacket is a necessity; a lightweight plastic helmet protects the head from rocks, and tile-setter's kneepads protect the knees from painful abrasions.

19: For a well-balanced canoe in a run of white water, paddlers kneel aft of the stern and bow thwarts. With the weight slightly aft, the bow rises a little.

The various strokes can be practiced in any kind of water, but it is in white water where they will be perfected; where the canoeist can watch the canoe react to his strokes; where the bow must be hooked to the right to avoid a sharp rock and the fast, hard draw stroke does the trick; where the canoe goes through a chute and is brought to a sudden stop by jam strokes at bow and stern and then is quickly pivoted to the right by fast back-paddling at the stern and a hard quarter sweep at the bow.

Capsizing is the major danger in white water. Properly equipped with helmet and life vest, the canoeist should not suffer more than bruises and wounded dignity. Unless you are in a cataract (and no advice is going to help anyone foolish enough to make a clearly suicidal attempt), a dunking in the rapids is usually just an exhilarating swim. Get away from the canoe if you can, relax, and go along with the water. After all, if you capsize, you are no longer canoeing, you are swimming through the rapids. Relax and enjoy yourself as much as you can. Your life vest will keep you up and your helmet will save your head from knocks. Work your way to shore and try again.

I once had a bad experience with a free stern line in a canoe capsize. I was under the canoe with my back jammed against a rock, and the force of the cascading water was slamming the canoe against me. But the major problem was that my feet and legs had become entwined in the long stern line that had been bunched under the stern deck behind the seat, and I couldn't get away from the canoe. I managed to force my head above water and shouted to my partner for help. He held me out of the water while I freed my feet and legs. Since then, I have never had a free line in my canoe. The lines, bow and stern, are neatly coiled around one side of the seat and tied off, that is one hazard I do not have to contend with.

It is never wise for a pair of novices in a single canoe to attempt white water where they are alone. Stay with a group. You will meet many people with similar interests and you will find safety in numbers.

## Canoe Camping

Canoe camping, once you get out of the canoe, is like any other camping, with two exceptions: In canoe camping, the sleeping bags are usually wet, and at least a third of your time is spent with a canoe on your back.

There are a few things the canoe camper should add to his regular camping equipment. Make sure you have sturdy, rubberized, waterproof bags to hold clothing, sleeping bags, cameras, etc. You will need extra paddles, a supply of drinking water, waterproof matches, and extra flashlight batteries. Sterno canned heat is easy to carry and lights whether wet or dry, so it comes in handy. Always take along a canoe-repair kit. If you are lucky, you won't have to use it, but it is good to know it is available.

Listed below is equipment suggested for a canoe camping trip for two.

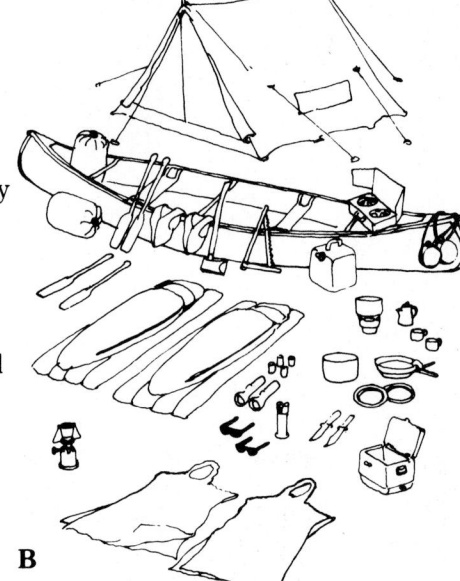

**B**

Figure B: Everything you need for comfortable canoe camping: Lightweight nylon mountain tent, lightweight (summer) sleeping bags with waterproof carrying bags, air mattresses, life jackets, extra paddles, hiker's ax, folding saw, plastic water jug (foldable), two-burner gas stove, canteens, cooking utensils (basket type), mess kits, flashlights, gasoline lantern, ponchos. For wilderness travel, it would be wise to include maps, compass, repair kits, first-aid materials, and a kit of emergency flares.

| | |
|---|---|
| Canoe | 2 ponchos |
| 4 paddles | Waterproof bags |
| 2 life jackets | 2 sleeping bags |
| Nylon tent | 1 ¾ woodsman's ax |
| 2 air mattresses | Folding saw |
| 2 mess kits | 2 flashlights; extra batteries |
| Coleman stove or Sterno | Insect repellent |
| Water can, 2 to 3 gallons | 2 canteens |
| 2 knives | Sunglasses |
| Cook set | Cooler (optional) |

My feeling is that if camping equipment cannot be carried in a pack, I don't want it. The cooler and Coleman stove would not be part of my gear. I also prefer a lean-to to a tent. Some campers like to take a radio along, but for myself I prefer the raucous wilderness.

For related entries see "Beachcombing," "Carryalls," "Clambakes," "Kayaks," "Piloting," "Sails and Sailing," "Shelters," "Survival Techniques," "Weather Forecasting."

# CANOEING CRAFTNOTES: FIBERGLASS REPAIR

1: First step in fiberglass repair is to cut out the area around the hole or fracture until all edges are smooth, solid fiberglass—even if this means slightly enlarging the hole. Major difficulty is cutting the hole in the canoe, but get in there with saber saw or jigsaw with a fine-tooth blade, and make the cut.

2: With sanding disk on an electric hand drill and coarse sandpaper (about 80-grit), sand the surface around the hole—on the inside of the hull—until the aluminum is sufficiently roughened to facilitate a good bond. The sanded area should extend at least 2 inches beyond circumference of the hole you have cut.

3: Next step is to cover hole from outside. Shape piece of aluminum or heavy cardboard to hull contour; cover with plastic wrap; place over hole, with plastic facing in, and secure it in place with masking tape.

4: Cut patches of fiberglass cloth and mat about 2 inches bigger than hole. Mix enough resin and catalyst (about 10 to 1) to wet both. Lay patches on plastic and saturate thoroughly with resin. Place mat over hole and cover with cloth. Put plastic wrap over area, and smooth out air bubbles with a putty knife; work out from center.

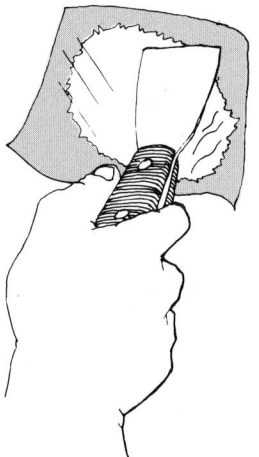

5: In one to two hours, remove cardboard from outside, and roughen surface around hole, feathering toward the inside. Mask area around the hole with heavy paper and tape to protect the finish. Cut a mat patch about 1 inch larger than the hole and several cloth patches about 2 to 3 inches larger. Mix a new batch of resin and catalyst.

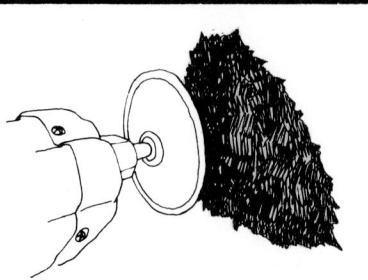

6: Brush resin into hole, and place mat patch over the hole. Mat will be stiff enough to maintain original contour. Saturate mat with dabbed-on resin. Apply a cloth patch, and saturate with dabbed-on resin. Keep adding cloth and resin until the layers are built up slightly above the hull's surface.

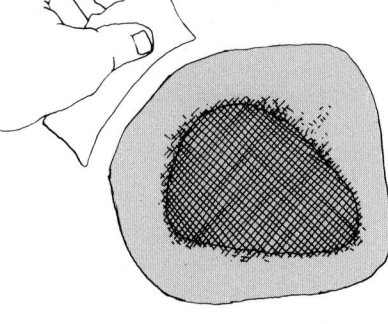

7: Smooth the patch, working all bubbles out to the edges, and let it cure about 20 minutes. When partially cured or rubbery to the touch, cut and strip off all excess cloth and mat on the outside edges of the feathering. Let the patch cure overnight (or about 12 hours), and then sand area until it is smooth and blends well with the undamaged area.

8: Mix color-matched gelcoat with resin, and apply to the repaired area, smoothing it with your hand or a squeegee. Cover the gelcoat with plastic wrap, and smooth again. Let the gelcoat cure completely; then rough-sand with wet, medium-coarse (about 220-grit) sandpaper. When the area is smooth to the touch, finish sanding with fine (about 600-grit) paper and buff thoroughly with rubbing compound until area matches original finish.

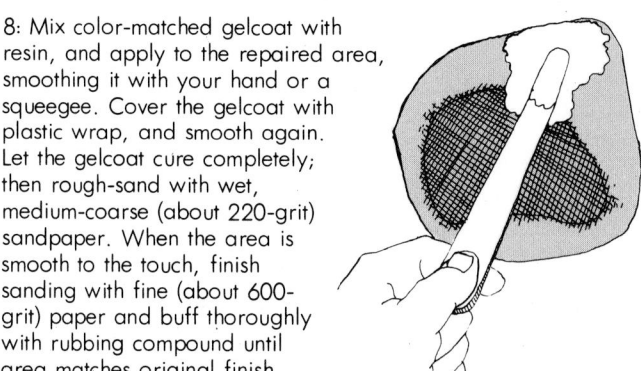

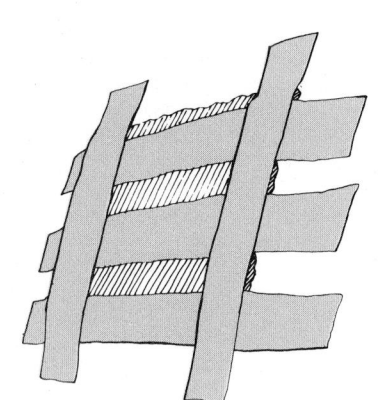

# CANOEING CRAFTNOTES: ALUMINUM REPAIR

1: Pound out damaged area to proper contour. If a crack is apparent, drill at each end with No. 30 drill to stop crack from running farther. Cut an aluminum patch larger than damaged area; form it to the curve of the area; draw a pencil line around it.

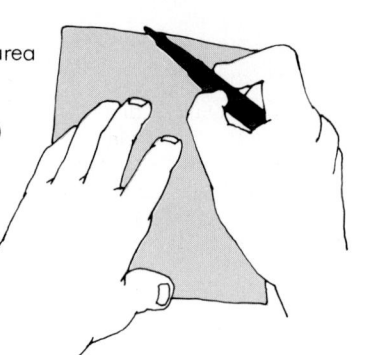

2: Remove the aluminum patch, and drill a hole in each corner. Size of the drill is determined by size of the pop rivets you will use. The size of the rivets is determined by the size of the hole you are patching. Fewer large rivets means drilling fewer holes. The corner holes should be about ½ inch in from the edges of the patch. With pencil and rule draw lines in the patch connecting the holes.

3: Guided by the penciled outline, place the patch back against the hull, covering the damaged area, and drill through the hull through one of the corner holes. Fasten the patch at this corner with a small bolt and nut to hold it in place. Then proceed to drill through the hull through the other three corner holes of the patch.

4: When the holes have been drilled in the hull through all four corners of the patch, it is secured to the hull by a bolt and nut in each corner. If you are using a No. 30 drill, the temporary fastenings should be ⅛-inch bolts with matching nuts. These locate plate so that the remaining holes can be drilled.

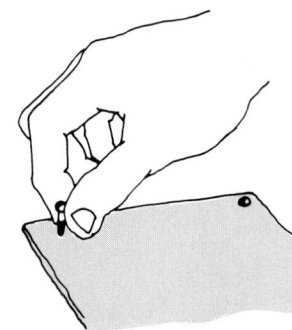

5: A pattern of holes with their centers an inch apart, go around the entire patch, drilling through the patch and the hull using the pencil lines on the patch as your guide. If it is an unusually large patch, drill a second row of holes an inch inside the first row, but staggered between the holes in the outer row. When all the holes have been drilled, the corner fastenings are removed and the patch is taken off the hull.

6: With a sharp, small-tooth file, remove the burrs from the holes on both sides of the patch and the inside and outside of the canoe. You can also hone down edges of the patch to make a better surface when the job is completed.

7: Spread a layer of marine caulking compound over the entire surface of the patch that will go against the hull of the canoe. This compound comes in small containers and is available at hardware and auto supply stores. It is a rubberized material that does not become hard and brittle and will ensure a water-proof bond between the patch and the hull. The patch is now put in place and fastened again at each corner with the temporary nut-and-bolt fasteners.

8: With a pop-rivet gun and closed-end pop rivets for a water-tight fit, patch is riveted progressively around the exterior. The temporary fastenings are removed, and those holes are riveted. The job is complete except for cleaning, smoothing, painting.

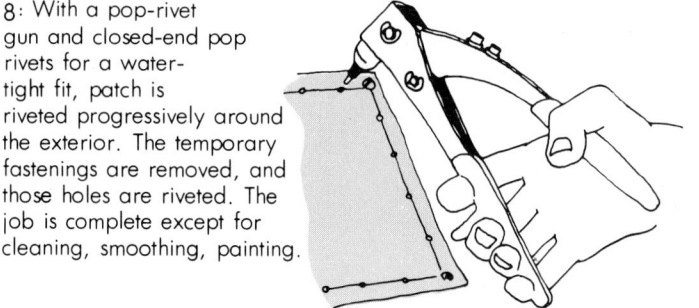

# CARDBOARD

# Tougher Than You Think

*Ron Lieberman is a graphic artist and illustrator free-lancing in New York City. Currently, he is working on book covers, magazines, record jackets.*

*Barbara Auran-Wrenn is a writer and crafts designer for magazines. She is also a contemporary folk artist and designs modernistic environments.*

As a crafts material, cardboard is surprisingly useful. With ingenuity and a few simple tools, it can be transformed into rugged and attractive furniture, toys, and many other things.

There are two kinds of cardboard. One is poster board, which comes in sheets and is used by manufacturers for gift boxes, oatmeal containers, and the like; it is generally useful for small projects. The other, corrugated, has a ribbed or fluted core faced on one or both sides with paper. It is used for packaging household goods, large appliances, and other large or heavy things. It is generally good for projects that call for strength.

Corrugated has an interesting history. Its invention in 1871 was really the beginning of the modern packaging industry. In all likelihood, the idea for the material evolved from the cuffs, collars, and petticoats worn by aristocrats in the sixteenth century. These accessories were fluted to make them stiff and bulky. In the nineteenth century, this fashion became popular when the advent of machines that greatly simplified the fluting process brought clothing with elaborate ruffles within the reach of the general public. From there, it was just a step—an ingenious one—to corrugated.

Corrugated owes its strength to the wavy-shape core or flutes, which give it bulk and rigidity. When corrugated is stood on end, the flutes act like supporting columns, and the strength is nothing short of amazing. You can make corrugated items that can hold hundreds of pounds. The table and stools on page 373, while more modest, can easily take the weight—and abuse—of children.

There are several types of corrugated. Single ply with one side faced with paper is good for projects where bending is required. Single ply with both sides faced is used where two finished sides are needed. Double ply (always double-faced) is used where considerable strength is needed. Corrugated is available at appliance stores and from paper manufacturers (see your telephone directory); poster board can be bought at art-supply stores. Both types of cardboard, of course, may be available around the home.

Tools and materials are easily obtained: scissors, mat knife, straightedge, white glue, pressure-sensitive cloth or plastic tape, white latex paint, ink roller (at art-supply stores), a small pane of glass. Also useful: a saber saw with a fine-tooth, metal-cutting blade for cutting heavier cardboard.

What makes this craft so intriguing is that you can act almost instantly on

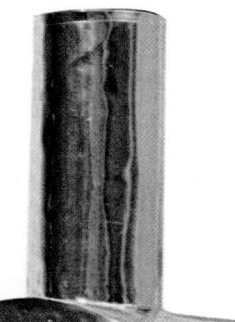

Shoe boxes on wheels, with an old-fashioned engine in the lead, make up the Ho-Ho Train. It can be as long as you wish. Directions, page 368.

an idea. For example, children love to play with boxes; so with a few decorations and some canned goods borrowed from the kitchen, they can convert a large carton into a store that will keep them amused for hours—and will encourage them to invent and make their own toys.

The ease and speed with which corrugated can be worked make it useful as a prototype material. If you are planning to buy new furniture, for instance, you can make simple scale models of the pieces and plan their arrangement before they arrive, thereby saving yourself a great deal of labor. Or if you are contemplating, say, a folding screen as a room divider and are not sure you would like it, just make a life-size mock-up to test its usefulness.

As you become more adept at working with cardboard, you will begin to recognize possibilities in all those boxes, mailing tubes, and other cardboard items that come into your home. For example, if you have several little boxes, you can make an attractive storage unit. Just spray the boxes with enamel paints of different colors, and glue the boxes in random fashion on a sheet of corrugated. Add a few pieces of cut-down mailing tubes; make some stripe accents with colored tapes, and there it is. You are sure to think of more ideas just as simple and useful.

Put your child in the arms of this headboard lady. Sides swing out for bedmaking. Directions, page 375.

## Toys and Games
# The Ho-Ho Train

Although this train is a toy, it also makes an amusing decoration.

Materials: Three shoe boxes in good condition; paper-towel tube; 3-inch-diameter mailing tube; 24-by-24-inch sheet of single-ply corrugated faced on both sides; 12-by-12-inch sheet of flexible poster board; ½ yard of self-adhesive vinyl paper in each pattern used; one box of cup hooks with screw eyes; 4 feet of ¼-inch doweling; white glue.

Use a shoebox for each car. See page 366 for vinyl patterns, and cover (photograph 1) sides, bottom, and lid of box for last car; inside and out of box for second car (lid is not used); only sides and bottom of box for engine; set lid aside.

Next, cut six axles from doweling, each 1 ¾ inches longer than box width. Insert screw eyes in boxes for axles (photograph 2). Cut wheels from vinyl-covered corrugated (photograph 3). See photograph 4 for installing axles and wheels. Set a compass to half the lid width (photograph 5). Draw two circles of this radius on plain corrugated. Cut out; score down center of each: attach to lid (figure A). These are the engine uprights. Measure and cut cover to go over uprights from poster board (figure A).

Make hole for paper-towel-tube smokestack one inch from front end and the diameter of the tube. Staple cover to lid; then secure smokestack in hole with tape.

Cut a 2-inch piece of mailing tube for the engine light. Cut a piece of vinyl to fit over engine front; cut a 2 ½-inch-diameter hole in vinyl's center. Make ½-inch cuts around hole edge; turn back resulting flaps. Adhere vinyl to engine front. Position tube in hole; secure it with flaps. Apply vinyl to engine where needed, and set assembly on box. Put last car's lid in place. Join cars with screw eyes and hooks.

1: When cutting the vinyl to cover boxes, overlap edges and corners. Also snip it with scissors where it starts to bunch.

2: To hold axles, insert and glue two pairs of screw eyes in box, each pair 2 inches from box end, eyes close to edge.

3: To make wheels, cover corrugated with vinyl; then mark and cut out 3-inch-diameter disks. Use a sharp mat knife.

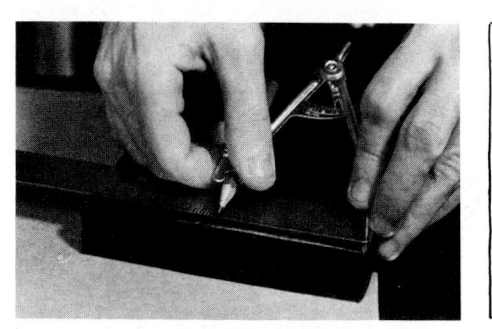

4: Slip axles through screw eyes. Punch hole in center of each wheel with pencil; push wheels onto axles as shown.

5: To get size of engine uprights, measure width of lid. Halve figure, and cut out corrugated discs to this radius.

**A** — Staple to lid edges — 4"

Figure A: Score discs down center; bend and staple to lid in position shown. From poster board, cut cover to size shown.

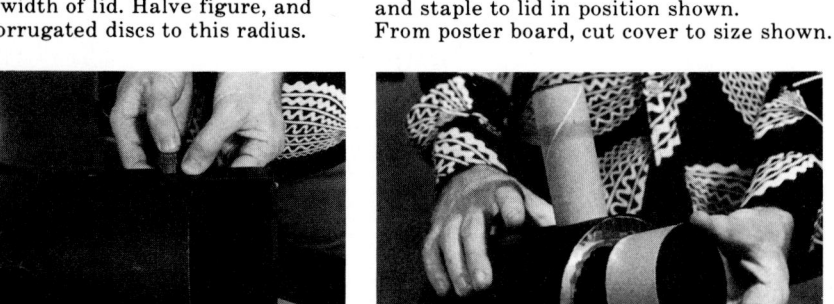

6: After making smokestack hole, bend cover over uprights, and staple to lid. Then insert and secure smokestack.

7: After covering front of engine with vinyl cut hole in center, stick light in place, secure with collar.

## Paper Folding and Cutting
# Whirligig

The whirligig is a modern derivative of the weathervane. When the wind hits it, the whole assembly turns, and the dog shakes hands with the girl. Materials needed are: two sheets of 26-by-36-inch corrugated faced on both sides; one sheet of 18-by-18-inch black flexible illustration board; ¼-inch-diameter plastic drinking straw; 2 feet of 18-gauge wire; paper clips; two fishing-line swivels; string; white glue; a pint of white latex paint; small bottles of red and white acrylic paint for decoration; 10 feet of 1 ½-inch-wide package-sealing tape.

First, use tracing paper and trace parts, which are shown actual size in figure B, page 370. Cut out patterns; outline them on black illustration board, and cut out. Set aside. Following figures D and E, page 371, cut out parts for vane and crankshaft housing (attached to one vane section; see figure D). Score vane pieces and crankshaft housing as indicated, except for end pieces on housing—these require fitting. Temporarily assemble the vane with tape. Fold the housing into its triangular shape (see figure F, top, page 371); fold the end pieces into position. Make sure they fit neatly into the housing, and trim if needed. Score as indicated; fold over housing, and tape temporarily in place.

As shown in figure E, make a centered, ¼-inch hole in each end of the housing to accommodate pieces of straw, which serve as bearings. Cut a 1-inch and a 4-inch piece of straw. As indicated in figure C, glue the 4-inch piece into the hole on the propeller end of the housing, letting it project 1 ¼ inches, so the propeller can clear the housing. Glue the 1-inch piece into the other end; allow to project only ¼ inch. Slip the wire through the bearings. Following figure D, bend it in the middle to form the crankshaft; bend it over at the nonpropeller mechanism (figure F, page 371). Slip one of the hubs over the wire. To make a spacer for the hubs, cut a 1 ¼-inch piece of straw; make ¼-inch cuts on each end all around; splay the piece at one end; slip it onto the wire; glue to the hub. Coat a 3- or 4-inch strip of paper, ¾ inch wide, on both sides with glue, wrap it tightly around the wire, and push it under the spacer. Let dry. Slip the other hub on the wire, and glue it in place so its slots are in the same position. Turn down the end of the wire. Then push the propeller blades into the slots at an angle, so they can catch the wind.

Assemble the dog and girl figures, using paper clips to attach the arms, as indicated in figure C. Split the tabs at the base of each, and, in turn, slip the bases into the slits at the top of the crankshaft housing. Fold the tabs in opposite ways, and glue to housing to keep the figures upright.

Straighten a large paper clip, or use a thin piece of wire, and poke it through the girl's hand and the dog's paw (figure C); loop in the wire to connect the paw and the hand loosely (the loop must be large enough so they can shake hands freely). Attach the other end of the wire to the center of the crankshaft with another loop.

The vane is now ready for final assembly. Glue 2-by-18-inch leading edge of black illustration board to one side of the vane (figure E) so it projects ½ inch. Apply glue to vane sections as shown in figure E; then position the string with the fishing-line swivels as shown in figure D. (The swivels will allow the assembly to rotate without the string's twisting.) Put vane sections together, and weight with books until dry. Then fold the crankshaft housing into shape, and secure with glue. Seal all edges with package-sealing tape, forming it over leading edge so it comes to a point. Paint all corrugated with latex. Decorate the whirligig with red and white acrylic paint as shown in the center photograph at right.

Follow figure H, page 371, to make brace, or wedge, that spreads vane wings. Hang the whirligig with a single string attached to the swivel at top. Run three strings from bottom swivel, and secure them to the floor.

*John Trull: Designer and art director, he now works in New York City as a free-lance artist and illustrator.*

Whirligig comes alive when the wind blows. The girl shakes the dog's paw, and the whole assembly gently rotates. It is not difficult to build.

Detail of the propeller mechanism. When the wind hits the blades, a crankshaft turns and a wire attached to it makes the paw and hand move.

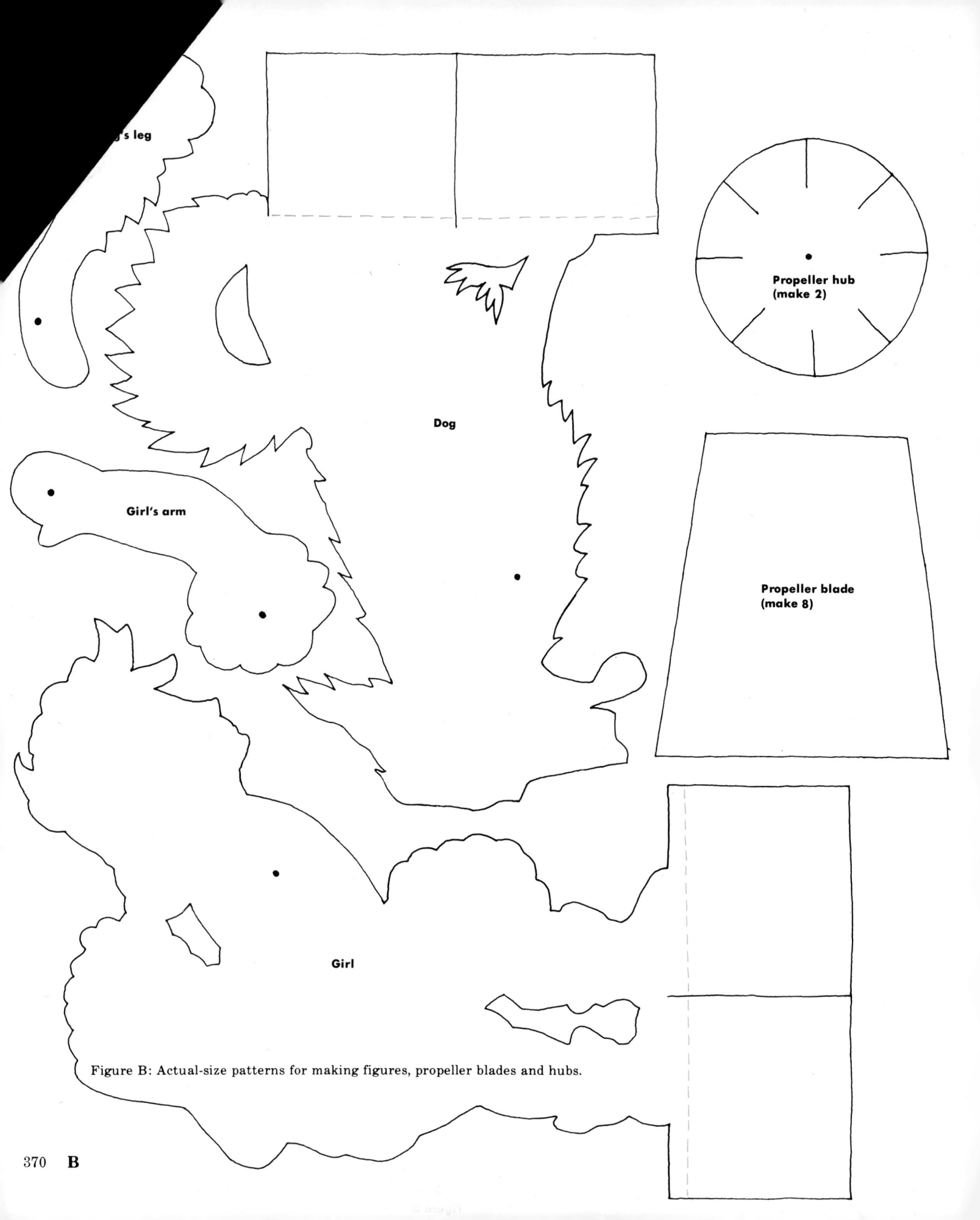

Figure B: Actual-size patterns for making figures, propeller blades and hubs.

Propeller hub
(make 2)

Propeller blade
(make 8)

Dog

Girl's arm

Girl

's leg

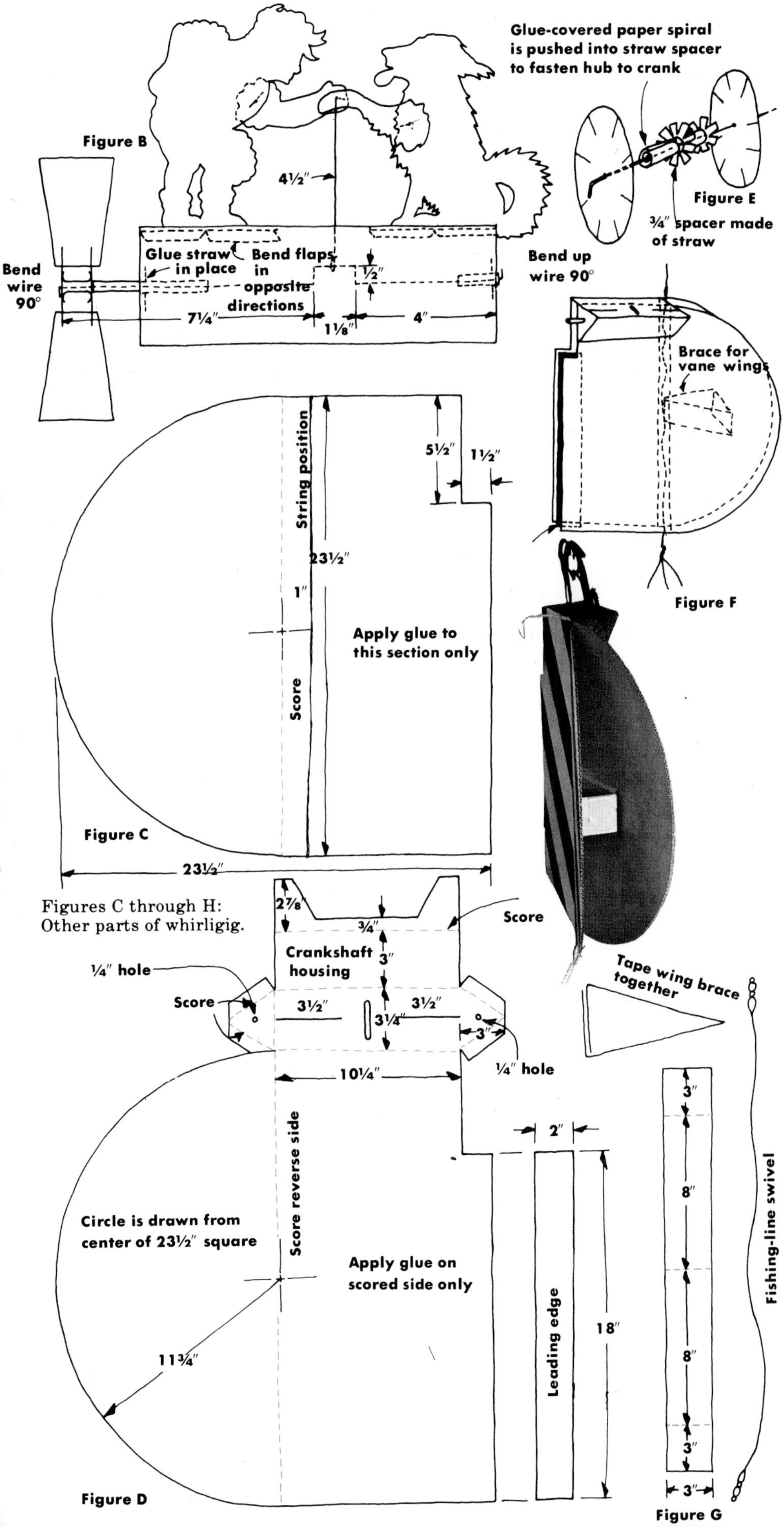

**Figure B**

Bend wire 90°

Glue straw in place

Bend flaps in opposite directions

4½″

½″

7¼″

1⅛″

4″

Bend up wire 90°

Glue-covered paper spiral is pushed into straw spacer to fasten hub to crank

**Figure E**

¾″ spacer made of straw

8: Cut the figures and propeller hubs and blades from this black illustration board. Make 16 blades and two hubs. Scissors cut board easily.

Brace for vane wings

**Figure F**

5½″

1½″

String position

23½″

1″

Score

Apply glue to this section only

**Figure C**

23½″

9: The crankshaft housing. When fitting ends, first fold them into position; then trim excess as needed to fit.

Figures C through H: Other parts of whirligig.

2⅞″

¾″

Score

¼″ hole

Score

Crankshaft housing

3″

3½″

3½″

3¼″

3″

¼″ hole

10¼″

Tape wing brace together

10: Close-up of the propeller hubs. Note ¾-inch spacer between the hubs and the portion of straw that projects from the end of the crankshaft housing.

Circle is drawn from center of 23½″ square

Score reverse side

Apply glue on scored side only

11¾″

2″

Leading edge

18″

3″

8″

8″

3″

3″

Fishing-line swivel

**Figure G**

**Figure D**

11: View of inside of crankshaft housing. Looped wire around the crankshaft extends through slot and connects with the dog's paw and the girl's hand.

*Richard Andrews, a graduate of Pratt Institute, is an industrial designer in New York City. At present, he is specializing in product design.*

*Paula Gulbicki also is a graduate of Pratt Institute, working in New York. Formerly a magazine craft designer, she now designs puppets and toys.*

# Cardboard furniture

Cardboard furniture, as mentioned earlier, need not live up to the idea it automatically brings to mind: flimsy and temporary. Well designed, it can last indefinitely and serve as well as regular furniture. But, unlike regular furniture, you can discard it without a qualm, because it is not expensive. As such, it might be just the thing for children. As they grow, you can make new furniture to fit their size.

## Tables and Stools

Materials: Nine 30-by-40-inch sheets of single-ply corrugated face on both sides; utility knife or single edged razor; masking tape; 2-inch wide and 1-inch wide rolls of orange, blue, and green pressure-sensitive tape; white glue; white latex paint; 2-inch nylon paint brush; one 13-ounce can each of orange, blue, and green enamel spray paint.

## Making the Tabletop

Cut 30-by-40-inch corrugated to these overall dimensions: tabletop top, 22 by 22 inches; tabletop bottom, 22 by 22 inches; table bases, four pieces, each 25 by 22 inches. Following patterns, Figure I, cut out tabletop bottom, top, and bases with the utility knife. Then score edges and corners (see photograph 12) on tabletop's bottom and top to make flaps. Make slots in bottom. Glue two of each base piece together for support and allow to dry, then cut tabs and slots.

Paint all sides of all pieces with latex to seal. Then, referring to the photograph on the opposite page for colors, give each piece two coats of enamel spray paint. Before spraying, it is a good idea to first practice on scrap cardboard. Hold the can about a foot from the cardboard surface, and move it across slowly. Do not hold the can in one spot. Rather, make a number of passes, trying for light, even coats rather than one heavy one. Let the first coat dry completely before you apply the second.

Now work on the top part of the tabletop. Following photographs 13 and 14, fold over flaps, and as you go, secure them in position with masking tape or glue, if you wish—forming a lip. Cover the lip with a continuous strip of 2-inch-wide tape. (See photograph for this and other tape colors.)

Assemble the base by sliding one piece into the other at the slots (see bottom sketch, figure I). Stick the tabs on the base through the slots in the bottom part of the tabletop. Fold over the tabs, and leave them unattached or glue them down. Fold over the edges on the bottom part of the tabletop, and slip it into the top part. Gluing is not necessary.

After assembly, outline exposed edges of base with 1-inch wide colored tape. The finished tabletop is 20 by 20 inches, with a base height of 22 inches.

12: Close-up of corner detail. Make all scores about ⅛ inch wide and deep enough to make folding over the flaps easy. Note that part of corner flap is cut free at one point.

13: Fold up flaps, as shown, at each corner. If the flaps do not fit well together, simply make wider scores or cuts as needed. Snug fitting means neat corners, essential if the piece is to look good.

14: After folding each corner, hold it together with masking tape. You can also use glue. When lip is formed, apply tape. You need 82 inches for tabletop lip, 66 inches for each stool.

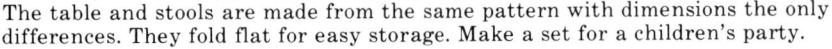

The table and stools are made from the same pattern with dimensions the only differences. They fold flat for easy storage. Make a set for a children's party.

## Making the Stools

The stools are simpler, smaller versions of the table. Follow patterns, figure I, and cut pieces to these overall sizes: top of stool 20 by 20 inches; bottom, 19½ by 19½ inches; base, two pieces, each 15 by 16 inches. Also, make the base slots 7 instead of 10 inches long, and the tabs and bottom slots 4 inches. Then simply follow the procedure for the table to make each stool. Refer to photograph above for paint and tape colors.

Keep the items (and this applies to any cardboard projects) away from direct heat. It attacks the glue and can weaken bonds.

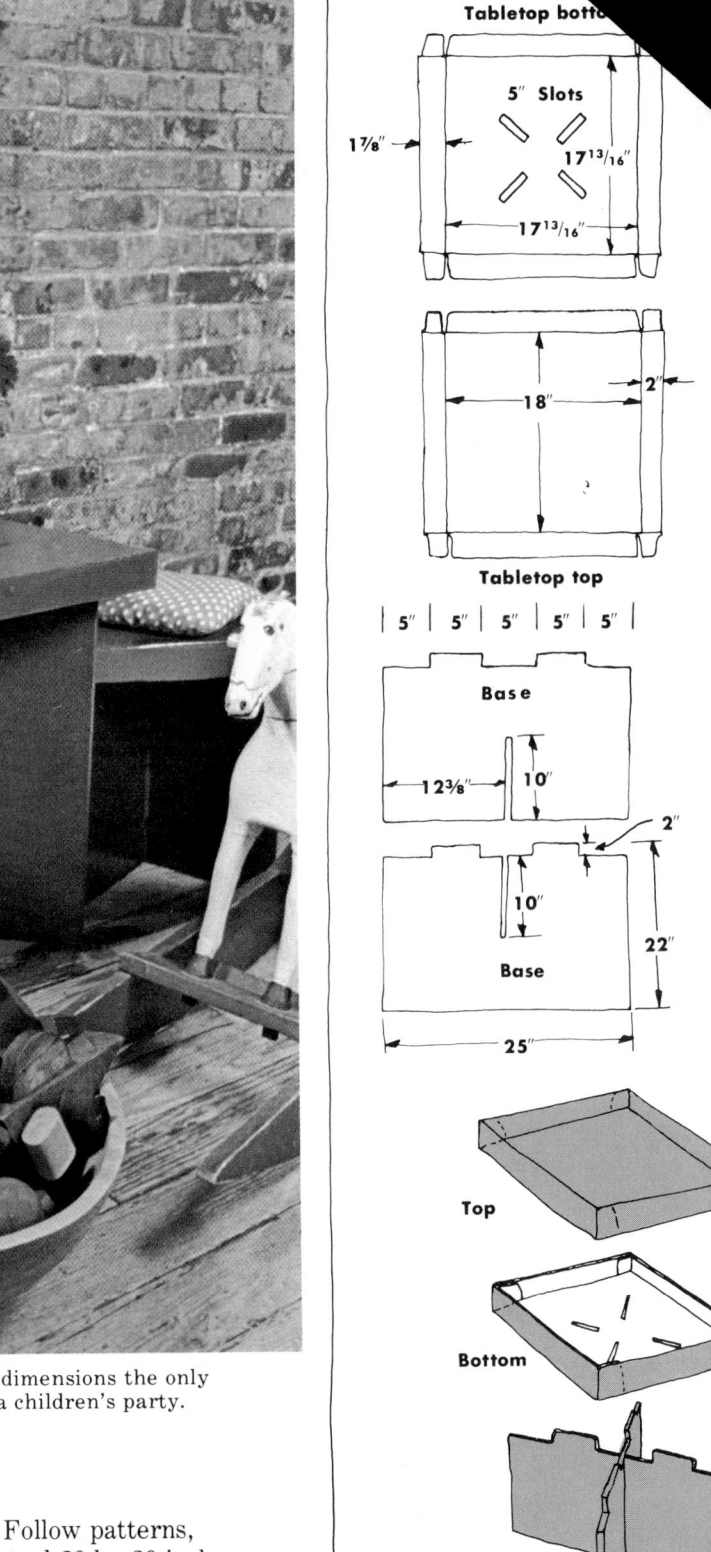

Figure I: Diagrams for corrugated table. A stool is made the same way. Its dimensions are given in the text.

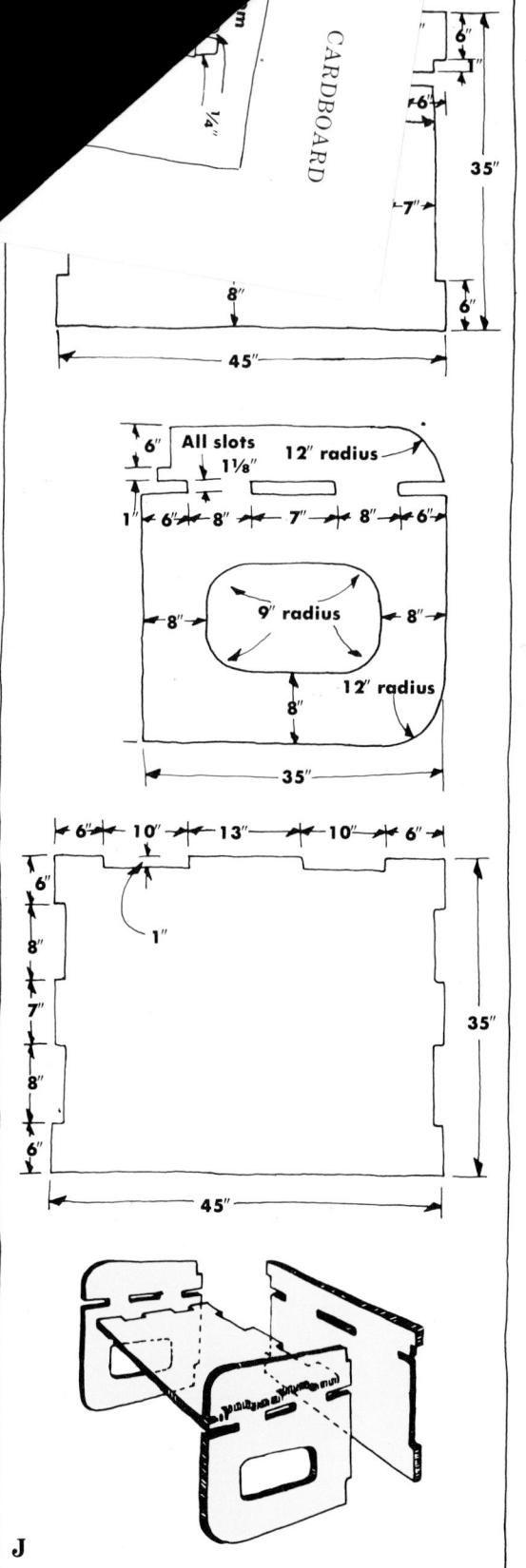

6"
6"
35"
7"
8"
6"
45"

6"  All slots  12" radius
1"⅛"
1"  6"  8"  7"  8"  6"
8"  9" radius  8"
12" radius
8"
35"

6"  10"  13"  10"  6"
6"
8"
1"
7"
8"
6"
45"
35"

**J**

Figure J: Patterns for back, sides, and top of corrugated desk. Exploded sketch at bottom shows how desk is assembled.

Construction of this corrugated desk involves an ingenious slot-and-tab method.

## Corrugated Desk

Materials needed are 17 48-by-48-inch sheets of single-ply corrugated faced on both sides; white glue; two quarts of white latex paint; 16 feet of ⅛-inch doweling; roll of 1-inch-wide gold plastic tape.

First, laminate corrugated (for this procedure, see headboard instructions, opposite) to make three sheets, each four layers thick, for the top.

Cut out back, top, and sides, following patterns, figure J.

Paint all sides of pieces to seal them; let dry. Then assemble desk as shown in exploded drawing, figure J. For strength, push doweling pieces into joints, as indicated by arrows. Cover exposed edges with tape.

# Headboard lady

This headboard, also pictured on page 367, is designed to fit a standard single bed. However, you can modify the dimensions to fit any bed.

Materials needed are two 48-by-48-inch sheets of double-ply corrugated; white glue; one quart of white latex paint; 45-by-48-inch piece of dotted cotton fabric; a roll of white 2-inch-wide pressure-sensitive tape; a 13-ounce spray can of orange enamel; two quarts of white enamel; medium-grade sandpaper; wood scraps; two 1-inch-diameter red buttons.

If you can't find double-ply corrugated cardboard, you can make double-ply from single-ply faced on both sides. Pour a good amount of glue on a small pane of glass. Using this as your roller pan, load an ink roller with glue, and evenly coat one side of one sheet. Lay a second sheet on it, with flutes of both at right angles and edges aligned. Weight; let dry overnight.

Headboard lady can become a masculine figure. Use the basic pattern and your imagination to make a figure suited to the decor of your room.

## Making the Headboard

To make headboard, first enlarge patterns, figure K (for procedure, see page 57, Volume One). Transfer to corrugated; cut out. Apply white latex paint to both sides of all pieces; let dry. Spray paint wig with orange enamel; paint arms and body with white enamel; let dry. Lightly sand with medium-grade sandpaper; wipe off dust. Apply a second coat of paint to parts.

Following figure K, cut cheeks from corrugated. Prime with latex; paint orange; glue on head. Glue on buttons for eyes, wood scraps for nose and mouth.

Trace shirt pattern on cotton fabric; cut out shirt. Apply glue to shirt area on body; attach fabric, smoothing out wrinkles. Let dry. To attach wig, first lay body flat. Apply glue to bottom of wig as needed; slip it under head; then weight down with books. To protect head, first cover it with waxed paper. Attach arms with short pieces of tape (see photograph for position). Cover exposed edges with tape.

For related projects, see "Boxes," "Models to Scale," "Puppets," "Toys." See also entries in the Index Volume under Furniture and Furniture Refinishing.

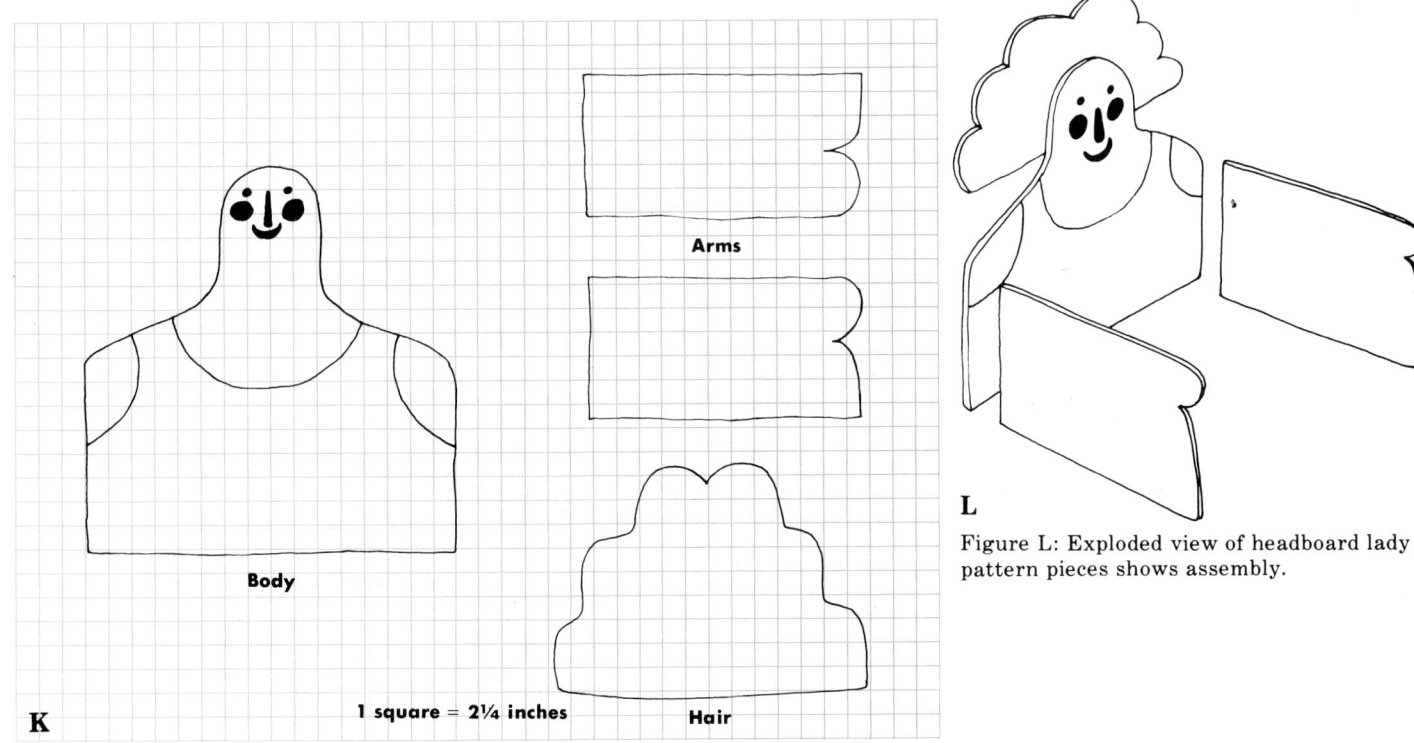

Figure L: Exploded view of headboard lady pattern pieces shows assembly.

Figure K: Patterns for body, arms and hair of headboard lady.

# CARD TRICKS

# When the Hand is Quicker

*Jeff Sheridan is a street magician and an expert card manipulator. He has performed card magic in the streets and parks of New York City since he was nineteen, and in 1972 he was the first magician to give a recital in Carnegie Hall. Jeff has also appeared at the Mercer Arts Center in Greenwich Village. His performances combine elements of magic, mime, and modern dance.*

Since the sixteenth century, magicians have used playing cards to intrigue and mystify their audiences. The first cards to appear in Europe during the Middle Ages were the *tarocchi*, or tarots. Royalty imported these decks for idle games of chance, but jugglers used them for *subtil manyement cartes*, sleight-of-hand tricks.

Of course, there have always been crooked gamblers. Many of the tricks we know today—using fixed decks, marked cards, and card-location systems— were practiced by shysters of previous eras. Gambling was so prevalent during the eighteenth century that cards were called the devil's picture books, and a cheater in England was punished by having his ears nailed to a pillory.

What the gambler did surreptitiously, the magician could do flamboyantly. Jean Eugene Robert-Houdin, sometimes called the father of modern magic, conjured cards for Parisian society during the 1840s and wrote *Gambling Swindles*, a thinly disguised account of his own tricks. S. W. Erdnase, in 1902, published a book called *Artifice, Ruse and Subterfuge at the Card Table*, which soon became a primer for neophyte magicians. During the 1920s and 1930s, Howard Thurston was famous for making cards leap through the air and vanish. And Harry Houdini, the great escape artist, first billed himself in traveling circuses as the King of Cards.

Modern magic is an art of invention, and I believe that each magician should develop a personal routine of deceptions and flourishes. The most

"Pick a Card" has long been part of the magician's routine. This eighteenth-century engraving shows a magician and his assistant, called the Merry Andrew.

The arm spread is a card manipulation that is sure to captivate an audience. Performing in the park, Jeff draws both children and adults to his show.

important rule is this: Never perform the same trick twice before the same audience. There are hundreds of stunts that can be done using the techniques of the mathematical and self-working tricks, the locator, the prearranged deck, and the sleight-of-hand. Magic tricks are deception and illusion used for the purpose of entertainment. Manipulating cards skillfully requires a great deal of practice. A good magician never repeats himself and never reveals his favorite tricks.

Two fans appear magically as Jeff
demonstrates with colorful flourishes.
For how to make a fan, see page 384.

One shot nailed a card to the wall in a trick performed by Joseph Pinetti during the late 1700s. Many later performers, including Robert Heller, imitated Pinetti's famous pistol trick.

## Glossary

**Break:** The cards are held apart to mark a location in the deck.

**Cold deck:** A stacked or prearranged set of cards, which is substituted for a normal deck during the performance.

**False shuffle:** The performer appears to mix the deck randomly, but preserves the order he needs for his trick (photograph 3).

**Flourish:** A visual display of card control. Typical flourishes are the arm spread (photograph 2), the fan, the giant fan, and the ruffle.

**Forcing:** Urging a spectator to draw a particular card or set of cards.

**Jog shuffle:** Accomplished by dropping cards, on edge, from one hand to the other in a random sequence.

**Lift:** Two or three cards are held separate and manipulated as though they were a single card (photograph 1).

**Misdirection:** An explanation or gesture by a performer that has the effect of misleading his audience.

**Palming:** Concealing a card in the palm of the hand.

**Participation:** Using members of the audience as assistants.

**Patter:** Conversation or monologue accompanying the trick.

**Spot cards:** Used to mark a location in the pack. Examples are the short card, the corner short, and cards with reversed designs.

1: The two-card lift. The performer uses the little finger of his left hand to separate the top two cards from the rest of the pile. The audience believes he is turning over a single card.

2: Arm-spread flourish. Spread the cards lengthwise from the palm of your hand to the crook of your elbow. With two fingers, reverse the direction of the cards, flipping them face up.

3: False shuffle. The deck is cut and given a two-handed shuffle. However, the performer gives the two halves a slight twist and separates them, laying the upper half on top again.

## Mathematical Tricks

Though the magician does not need to perform supermental calculations, he can mystify an audience by appearing to control random events. Mathematical tricks usually depend on convenient formulas or special arrangements of the cards rather than on the mental powers of the performer. In the mind-reading trick pictured on the opposite page, the magician needs to remember only the positions of the two odd cards.

Since a mathematical trick can be solved logically, it is important to work this one smoothly and quickly. The effect should be performed only once, without preparing the audience for the outcome.

**Mathematical Mind Reading:** The audience believes there are six possible choices, but the performer knows there are only two.

In preparation, lay six cards on a table in the order shown in photograph 4. The audience does not realize there is only one card with a blue back, the third from the performer's left. And there is only one card from a red suit, the second from his left.

The performer claims that he can always find the odd card with the help of a member of the audience, and he asks an observer to choose a number between one and six. No matter what the number is, it leads the performer to the odd card. Photographs 5 and 6 demonstrate how this is done.

Note: In all tricks, instructions are from the performer's viewpoint.

4: Viewing the cards on the table, the audience assumes that all are from the same deck, with red backs. If a spectator calls out "Two," count over two positions from the left. Since this card is face down, turn it over. Then turn all the cards face up. If a spectator calls out "Five," count over five from the right. This brings you to the same position. "Do you want me to turn it over?" you ask the spectator. When he says "Yes," turn all the cards face up.

5: Pointing to the chosen card, you say, "Look, you chose the only red card." Then collect all the cards face up, return them to the pack, and you are ready to perform the next trick. However, the first time the trick is done, the spectator may call out "Three" or "Four." If the number is three, count from the left. If the number is four, count from the right. This brings you to a face-up card. Turn the other cards face down; then turn over the chosen card.

6: "Look, you chose the only blue card," you say. Make sure the cards remain face down as you return them to the deck. At the beginning, you should emphasize that the number must be between one and six. If someone in the audience has made the mistake of saying "One" or "Six," you can still achieve the effect shown at the left. Starting from your left, spell out "S, I, X" or "O, N, E," counting one card for each letter. Arriving at the third position as before, reverse all the cards that are face up.

8: Cut the deck, and place the top half in front of the audience. Since the queen of clubs was retained on top, that card will be discovered by the spectator.

9: Studying the top card on your own pile, announce to the audience that the spectator is holding the queen of clubs. Place your pile on top, and jog shuffle.

### Self-Working Tricks

These can be done with a normal deck, and they do not require advanced skill in manipulation. Often, patter is very important. You can make a trick seem comic, accidental, or mysterious according to how you describe the effect that is taking place. For Mini Mind Reading, I like to suggest that there is a secret relationship between the two top cards.

**Mini Mind Reading:** Perform the shuffle shown in photograph 7, noting the top card. Cut the deck toward the audience (photograph 8). Ask the spectator to look at the top card on his pile (photograph 9). Study the top card on your own pile, and announce the spectator's card.

7: The top card may be retained during the jog shuffle, as shown here. Separating the uppermost card with the little finger of the left hand, shuffle the rest of the cards in a normal manner.

10: "Here are the four burglars," you say as you display the four jacks. It appears to the audience that these are the only cards in your hand.

11: In fact, three dummy cards are hidden behind the jack of diamonds, as shown here. All seven cards are then placed face down on top of the deck.

12: Insert the top cards into the deck, saying, "One burglar goes in the basement and one on the ground floor, one on the second floor and one in the attic." The fourth card may be shown to the audience.

13: Deal the four jacks from the top as you say, "All the burglars come out in the attic." Of course, the first three burglars were the dummy cards, and they are now mixed in the pack.

14: The jack of diamonds is the locator, since it is on the bottom of the deck. Note this card after the deck has been shuffled and before the trick begins.

**Burglars' Meeting:** "Burglars always come together in the end," you claim. "And I can prove it." Select seven cards from the deck, the four jacks plus three dummy cards, which are hidden by the last jack (photographs 10 and 11). Place the cards on the deck. As your patter continues, insert the dummy cards in the deck, one near the bottom, two near the middle. The fourth card, the only jack that changes place, goes among the other jacks on top. Now you are ready to deal all four jacks from the top (photograph 13).

### Using a Locator

**The Magic Pencil:** Shuffle the deck thoroughly, and note the bottom card, which is the locator. The locator's position is shown in photograph 14. Spread the cards face down, and ask a spectator to draw any one. Cut the deck as shown in photograph 15. Ask the spectator to place his card on the pile in your left hand. Replace the top cut.

Spread the cards face up on the table, and pass a pencil back and forth above them, asking the spectator to concentrate on his card. The pencil will find his card directly above the locator (photograph 17).

A woodcut of the ace of spades displays card maker's inscription and city scene.

15: The deck is cut by holding the upper half in your left hand and drawing out the lower half with thumb and middle finger of the right hand. Make this cut after a spectator has chosen a card.

16: The spectator replaces the chosen card between the two halves of the cut deck. In this photograph, the locator is on the bottom of the pile held in performer's right hand.

17: Passing a magic pencil over the surface of the cards, you first note the position of the locator. Point the pencil at the card overlapping the locator. That is the chosen card!

## The Prearranged Deck

Stacking the deck was a gamblers' ruse, and many exposes have been written about their arrangements. One method was to shuffle a normal deck, set it aside, and call for drinks. When an accomplice waiter came to the table, he was holding a cold (stacked) deck under his tray. He left the cold deck, picked up the shuffled one, and the gambler dealt himself a royal flush.

Magicians have developed complicated formulas for prearranged decks. One, described by Erdnase, was a rotational system revealed by the jingle: "Eight kings threatened to save Ninety-five queens from one sick knave." Each syllable suggested a different card in the order.

Easy-up is done with the simplest of prearranged decks.

**Easy-up:** Separate all red cards from black cards in the deck. The arrangement can be seen in photograph 18. Holding the cards face down, begin pushing them from your right hand into your left. This should be done slowly, while you are insisting that the spectator can draw any card. In fact, your arrangement forces the spectator to draw a card from the upper half of the deck, and you know it must be a black card.

Have him replace his card. Again, display the cards face down, moving them slowly from one hand to the other. This time, you are offering him the bottom portion of the deck, retaining the upper half in one hand.

When the spectator has replaced his card, ask him to concentrate while you go through the deck and try to pick up vibrations. Of course, the chosen card will be the only black card in the red half of the deck (photograph 19). When you come to it, cut the deck, transferring the lower cut to the top.

Now for the easy-up. Straighten the deck, and raise it, face down, 2 or 3 feet above the table. As you do so, slide the top card forward until it is nearly halfway over the edge of the deck. Quickly drop the cards to the table. The chosen card will be the only one to flip face up.

18: In the prearranged deck shown here, the red suits are on performer's right, the black suits on his left. When the deck is turned face down, all the black cards will be on top. The spectator is forced to take a card from the upper half and to replace it in the lower half.

19: Only one card is out of place, the eight of clubs. The performer knows this was the chosen card. To prepare for the easy-up, he will next cut the pack between the eight of clubs and six of hearts, leaving the chosen card on top.

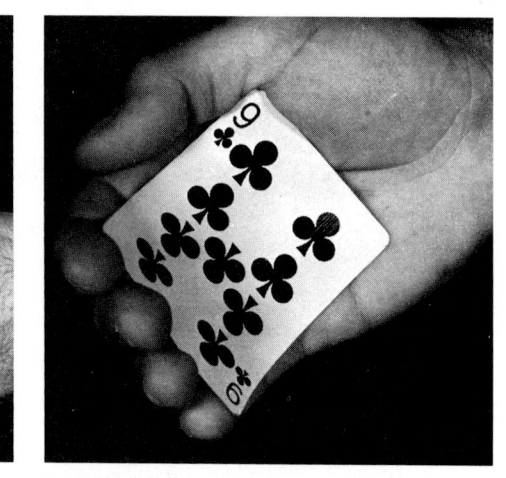

20: The palm is used for Conjuring a Card (see opposite page). First, slide the top card forward with the fingertips. As the edge of the card tilts upward, cup the palm of the hand to receive it.

21: Spring the card inward with the fingertips and lower part of the thumb. So it won't look unnatural, hand should be curved only enough to keep the card sprung tightly against the palm.

## Sleight-of-Hand

Sleights are the most difficult, because they require some proficiency in card manipulation. They are most effective in creating the illusion of magical appearance and disappearance. For conjuring a card, I have demonstrated two sleights used by every magician, the palm and the back palm. Before trying to conjure a card, you should practice both of these manipulations, which are demonstrated in photographs 20, 21, 22, and 23.

**Conjuring a Card:** Display the cards face down. Tell the audience that you are going to let someone choose a card and that, just to make sure there will be no cheating, he can replace the card anywhere he wants to. Then

22: The back palm is a more advanced method of concealing a card, and it is also more difficult. To begin, hold the card as in this photograph. Then stretch out your two middle fingers.

23: When your hand is outstretched, the card is concealed from the audience. To conjure the card, release its lower edge, and tilt the hand forward. The card will spring into view.

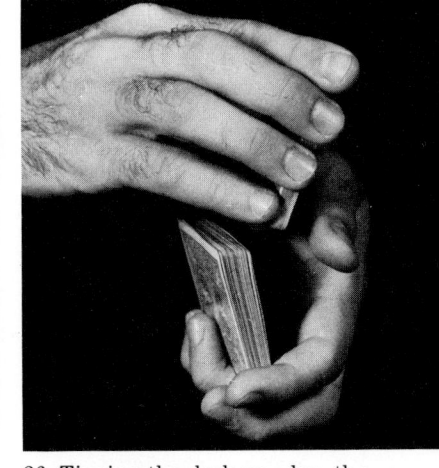

24: "Take any card," you tell the spectator. When he replaces the card, however, you mark a break in the deck. Slide the little finger just above where the spectator has placed the card. Note that your fingers are conveniently hidden by the spread of cards.

display the cards from hand to hand, as in the previous trick (see photograph 24), until the spectator selects one.

As the spectator replaces the card, slide the little finger of your left hand above it, to mark it. This sleight should be executed so that it cannot be seen by the audience.

While you straighten the deck, maintain the break with your little finger, as shown in photograph 25. This maneuver also should be concealed from the audience.

Now cut the deck. Hold the cards upright in your left palm. With the right hand, lift all cards below the break, and drop them to the outside of the cards in the left hand (photograph 26).

The chosen card is now on top and is ready to be palmed. Since your

25: With the top of the deck facing the audience, maintain a break directly above the chosen card, which the spectator has replaced. Note that the fingers of the left hand are raised around the edges of the deck to conceal the break.

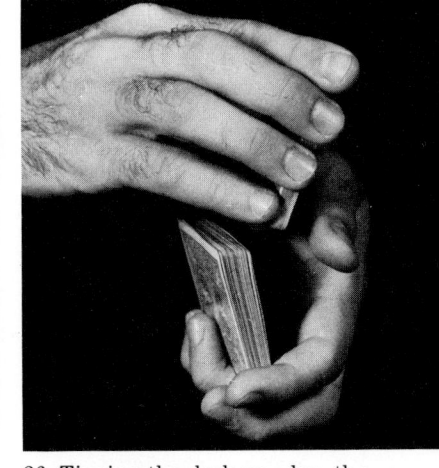

26: Tipping the deck on edge, the performer lifts all the cards that are below the break and places them on top of the pile. Since the little finger returns to position, this appears to be a perfectly normal cut.

hands are close together, it is easy to press the card into your palm, as you can see in photographs 20 and 21. With more practice, you can conceal the top card behind your hand, using the technique for the back palm demonstrated in photographs 22 and 23.

Hand the deck to the spectator, and ask him to find his card. After he has searched in vain for a moment or two, you can pluck the card from behind his ear (photograph 27) or out of his shirt pocket.

27: With the palmed card in hand, reach behind the spectator's ear and snap the card into view. The audience will be distracted by the spectator searching the deck for his chosen card. Apparently, you have conjured it out of the air.

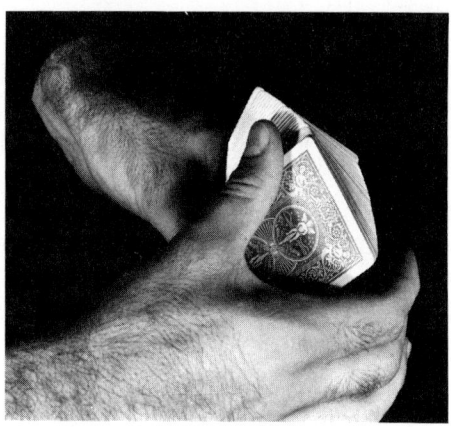

28: The cards are held firmly but loosely in the left hand. The first and second fingers hold the lower edge of the deck, while the ball of the left thumb applies a steady pressure.

29: Press the thumb of the right hand against the edge of the deck until the cards begin to turn. Spread the cards by moving the right thumb toward the top, using the left thumb as a pivot.

30: When the right thumb reaches the top card, the fan should be complete. Note that the cards are evenly spaced and form an almost complete circle. With practice, you can make the fan in an instant.

## The Flourish

With a deft card flourish, you can demonstrate your mastery of the cards and also draw the attention of a sizable audience. One warning, however: This kind of card manipulation requires the most practice. Don't expect to produce a perfect fan the first time you try it.

**Making a Fan:** As a street performer, I have to make large displays with the cards in order to attract an audience. I usually end each performance by producing a number of colorful fans "out of thin air." Photographs 28, 29, and 30 show how to make the simplest fan, using both hands. When you have mastered that, try the giant fan pictured below. Begin by inserting the bottom of a second deck into the top of the first, alternating red and blue cards. Then apply pressure with the right thumb to open the fan.

For related entries, see "Birthday Celebrations" and "Magic."

31: The giant fan needs two decks. Insert bottom of a red deck into top of a blue deck, alternating cards throughout. Pressure is applied at top of the blue cards.